THE Wisdom OF Donkeys

Finding Tranquility in a Chaotic World

❦

ANDY MERRIFIELD

BLOOMSBURY
NEW YORK · LONDON · OXFORD · NEW DELHI · SYDNEY

Bloomsbury USA
An imprint of Bloomsbury Publishing Plc

1385 Broadway	50 Bedford Square
New York	London
NY 10018	WC1B 3DP
USA	UK

www.bloomsbury.com

BLOOMSBURY and the Diana logo are trademarks of
Bloomsbury Publishing Plc

First published by Walker & Company in 2008
This paperback edition published in 2010

ISBN:	HB:	978-0-8027-1593-7
	PB:	978-0-8027-1992-8
	ePub:	978-0-8027-1872-3

Library of Congress Cataloging-in-Publication Data is available.

13

Typeset by Westchester Book Group
Printed and bound in the U.S.A. by Sheridan
Chelsea, Michigan

To find out more about our authors and books visit www.bloomsbury.com.
Here you will find extracts, author interviews, details of forthcoming
events and the option to sign up for our newsletters.

For Corinna

DOGS, CATS, AND horses are the subject of innumerable popular books. Less common are books about birds and wild mammals. Very rarely are other animals, especially domestic animals, considered sufficiently important to study, let alone to honor with serious nonfiction. Yet here is one of the best animal books of our time, and it's about a donkey. Yes, a donkey—a sensitive, knowledgeable, graceful donkey with "dainty legs and little hooves," as is true of any donkey. Thus one of the most rewarding things about this splendid book is that it totally and successfully counters the malignant reputation of these enchanting animals—that they are stubborn or stupid or bad tempered. They are none of those things. If they seem so on certain occasions, it is only because they are trying to protect themselves from human cruelty.

I am fascinated with donkeys and have been ever since I witnessed a remarkable scene near a Namibian village. One of the villagers owned a little donkey whose front feet were hobbled so he couldn't run away. As a result, he had to move both front feet together. In that extremely rural part of Africa there were no barns or fenced pastures, not even paddocks. By day and by night, the domestic animals took their chances on the open veldt. I worried about the donkey because the local water hole was shared by lions, and not only was the donkey unprotected by his owner, he also seemed unable to protect himself.

One day a feral horse appeared—a stallion. He galloped freely here and there, tossing his head. He noticed the donkey grazing peacefully under a tree, took exception to his presence, and charged. He was at least three times as big as the donkey, and seemed very ferocious as he rushed up to attack, when suddenly, *wham!* The donkey let fly his hind legs in a kick that had it connected would have sent the horse up in the air. The horse backed off, astonished. The donkey went on grazing. The horse ran around for a while with his eyes on the donkey, then convinced himself that despite his first attempt, a little, hobbled donkey must be vulnerable, and he attacked again. This time the donkey planted himself on his bound front feet as if in a headstand and aimed the whole force of his body at the horse's chin. The horse tossed his head so the kick missed by inches, but the horse must have felt a powerful wind from the donkey's hind feet. The horse backed off and the donkey went on grazing.

It then became clear why the donkey had positioned himself under a tree. The horse, or any other attacker, had to approach from the rear. The horse saw this, too, and circled the tree to try to get the donkey from the front. But the donkey well knew what the horse had in mind and kept the tree between them. At this point I tried to find the owner of either the donkey or the horse, but neither was present, so I could only watch in amazement for the next few hours while the little donkey defended himself with all the skill and wisdom of his strong, heroic species.

Much as I would like to, I don't know the fate of that courageous little donkey. I only know that a few days later, he was grazing peacefully under another tree, uninjured, and the horse had gone away.

The episode left me with a towering respect for donkeys, and when I was asked to write a foreword for a book about a donkey, I could hardly wait to oblige. And that was my good fortune, because the book is riveting in its account of an enviable journey with an equally magnificent donkey through the Auvergne region of France. On that memorable journey, Andy Merrifield was able to recall his own fascinating life, and to contemplate, in a most illuminating manner, many important aspects of history, science, literature, and art. Having majored in literature in college and grad school, and having been a writer and an English teacher for most of my life, I thought I knew something about literature, but I found I didn't have a patch on Merrifield, from whom I feel I've learned enough to get another advanced degree. Very few of us have a patch on Merrifield, and just about anyone fortunate enough to be reading this book will emerge at its conclusion significantly better educated than he or she was at the start. A great treat lies in store.

A second great treat will be the trip through the Auvergne region, so well described that one all but takes the trip oneself. But the greatest treat in store is Gribouille, the intelligent, sensitive, serene little donkey who carried Merrifield's pack. Merrifield learned almost as much from Gribouille as we can learn from Merrifield. For some, this will come as a surprise. We have all kinds of erroneous preconceptions about virtually every animal that comes to our attention—dolphins love us and want to make us happy; pigeons are a pestilence; cheetahs are friendly, so we all should own one; rodents are unsanitary; horses are noble, fit for kings; donkeys lack class and are only fit for unwashed peasants. But these are just our perceptions, and as usual, because our culture can be incredibly inaccurate when it comes to animals, the perceptions are all wrong.

None more so than our perception of donkeys. In reality, they are remarkable animals, stronger and more adaptable than horses, able to live where horses cannot, and with substantially more endurance, so that tasks that would murder a horse are readily performed by donkeys. They are superior to humans, too, in a number of ways. Their senses are more acute than ours (although that's no surprise). Yet it is their calmness, their serenity, their self-knowledge and confidence that put us to shame. Thus this book is a lesson in calmness and sureness. Can we improve our psychological climate by emulating a donkey? Of course we can.

—Elizabeth Marshall Thomas
October 2009

1

I CAN'T STOP thinking about Schubert. Piano sonata number 20. Its haunting melancholy is lodged in my brain as I pedal toward the sky. Schubert's slow, precise, sparse cords syncopate with my own slow pumping and deep gasps for breath. I'm listening to the music of greenness, no radio necessary. The somber sounds are surprisingly uplifting in the afternoon sunshine. I'm riding a bike near my home in France's Auvergne region, up a high mountain pass. I ride when it isn't too cold, before the snow arrives. The narrow route wends its way up and up through tiny hamlets made up of stone cottages, abandoned barns, the odd menacing dog, and clucking hens: Le Chambon, Le Bancillon, and Channat. These are real places, at least they seem real to me, with a temporality that ticks in a Middle Age time warp.

It's hard going up the mountain, easy to lose traction on dry gravel paths splattered with cow dung. Yet I'm rewarded at the summit with a sweeping vista across the valley, and I can see the Allier River down below. Hills undulate and interpenetrate, float away in the misty warmth. The peace is serene, the silence dulcet music. The meadows are a natural auditorium; its acoustics are razor-sharp. Around the bend I go. A meadow opens itself to the world. The music inside me is a sonata, but the landscape outside is a symphony. Up here Schubert comes into his own, Franz Schubert, who created masterpieces while still a teenager. He died at such a tender age, at thirty-one, already fifteen years my junior. I stop and dismount against a tree, a particular tree, the tree around the bend. I've spent hours stopped at this spot, just looking, staring across the valley, surveying planet Earth. The slope is steep, an almost-45-degree gradient, and the grass below is worn and full of tufts and bracken. For half the year it's home for a dozen or so chocolate-colored and turtledove-gray donkeys.

There's something amazing about watching donkeys graze in the middle of nowhere. It's a kind of therapy, even a sort of meditation. You can both lose and find yourself. An Australian proverb says that when you watch donkeys in a meadow, don't forget your chair. You can observe them for hours on end—it's hypnotic and addictive. It's hard to drag yourself away once you're smitten. All you hear is a faint rustle as they shuffle through the grass and bury their heads in the earth, chomping away. This faint rustle is exclusively donkey, their own private language game, an utterly different sound from a flock of sheep or goats, and different again from a field of horses or cows. Donkeys are both grazers and browsers: their teeth and lips let them graze near to the ground, trawling the earth close-up for food; their narrow muzzles allow them to browse with great sensitivity, foraging quality rather than just quantity.

Donkeys' legs are beguiling: their knees and shanks, fetlocks and hocks, cannon bones and pastern joints are so dainty and graceful, so slender. Horses' legs look clumsy in comparison. It's unbelievable the load these little legs can bear, unimaginable for any human. No horse could ever pace up a narrow mountain pass carrying a donkey's load, could do it so assuredly or confidently, so reliably or patiently. Horses are faster, yet have much less endurance than donkeys, and are nowhere near as agile. They're edgier, too, especially in tight situations. They bolt whereas a donkey freezes. You can usually cajole an anxious horse to do things against its better interests, frighten them into galloping along hazardous, unsafe routes. Not so with donkeys, who have a highly developed sense of self-preservation. Thus a donkey's perceived stubbornness.

One of a donkey's best-known characteristics is its bray. This noise can really carry, sometimes for a distance of two miles. They bawl out and the bray echoes across the airwaves, apparently in seven different tonalities, from partial eeyore calls to full-repertoire braying; donkeys can vocalize on both inward and outward breaths, expending a massive amount of energy doing so. In the countryside, down in any valley, a donkey's bray will rattle neighboring villages. Donkeys bray when they're happy or unhappy, when they're communing with a mate, when they're feeling lonesome, or when they know food is near and about to arrive. Occasionally, they'll bray just for the hell of it, yell at the top of their voices, let it all go for a while, for fun. Then they'll roll about on their backs in the earth, do it together as a group, take a soil bath in Mother Nature.

They're gregarious animals and like company; they don't seem to mind me here, the curious uninvited guest, the small-eared visitor who has come up the mountain to learn.

At first the donkeys paid me little attention, giving only occasional, disinterested glances in my direction, too preoccupied with their meal and their quiet thoughts. After several weeks of returning to the same patch, some eventually ventured up the slope. With upright, inquiring ears and curious, petitioning eyes, they'd give me melancholy stares. They seemed so utterly calm and gentle. Under their frizzy fronts and impenetrable gaze, behind their dark, nonjudgmental eyes, I sensed deep philosophical thoughts as well as a tacit fraternity—the fraternity of a chance meeting on a summer's afternoon, the vulnerability of two finite beings in illicit rendezvous.

❧

Time slows down amid donkeys. In their company things happen quietly and methodically. It's hard to forget their innocent gaze. It's a calm that instills calm. Your mind wanders, you dream, you go elsewhere, yet somehow you remain very *present*. Milan Kundera says in his novel *Slowness* that speed, the demon of speed, is often associated with forgetting, with avoidance, and slowness with memory, with confronting. We move slowly when we want to listen to ourselves, to others, and to the world around us. We move slowly when we want to confront ourselves. If only we could slow down! The rush of contemporary life overwhelms our ability to observe, to hear, to step back and wonder, and to meditate. Our society, Kundera says, wants to blow out the tiny trembling flame of memory. The birds are still chirping, yet the sun is disappearing now over the hills. There's a far-off tractor in a field surrounded by mounds of hay bales. The rush of contemporary life is a universe away these days.

A couple of donkeys amble toward me and poke their muzzles over the wire fence. I rub their foreheads and caress their ears. The thick fur on their brow is supersoft and inexplicably warm. I push down on the rump of one donkey, on his croup: it feels absolutely rock solid, unmovable and unflappable. More follow up to the fence, jockeying one another for a pat. They're content and so am I, more content than I ever was in any frenzied throng; I'm rediscovering myself up a mountain, in silent company. When a dog is happy he wags his tail; donkeys prick up their ears. If their ears are tucked down, you know something's up. A Jacques Prévert verse comes to mind: "Oh, gray donkey, my friend, *mon semblable mon frère,*/ As perhaps Baudelaire might have said ... Look at the donkey, messieurs/ Look at the gray donkey,/ Look at its regard,/ men of great knowledge ..."

"They're queer, pale things, these humans," I remember the donkeys saying in another Prévert ditty, "The First Donkeys." "They walk on two legs, their ears are very small, and they're not so handsome." The French poet was talking about us, the ugly ones, and empathizing with those creatures with big floppy ears and frizzy fringes. "Long ago, donkeys were absolutely wild; they ate when they were hungry, they drank when they had thirst, and they ran in the grass to their hearts' content." Ah, but one day, in the land of the donkeys, "the kings of creation" arrived, for "that's how we men like to think of themselves." The simple donkeys were very content with all this, so they trotted up to meet the humans. We'll give them a little reception, said the donkeys, merrily.

But only a few minutes after arriving, "the kings of creation had tied all the donkeys up like sausages." All, except the youngest donkeys, were put to death and roasted on a spit. The humans began eating, yet soon grimaced angrily. "That doesn't rank with beef!" one man said. "It's not good, I prefer lamb!" said another. "Oh, this is awful," shouts somebody else. Then the men start to cry. "And the donkeys in captivity, seeing the humans cry, think it's remorse that brought on the tears." "They'll free us now," the naïve donkeys believe. But the humans get up and speak together and make grand gestures. "These animals aren't nice to eat, their cries are disagreeable, their ears are ridiculously long, they are surely stupid and don't know how to read or count. We'll call them 'donkeys,' because such is our whim and they'll henceforth carry our bags. For it is us, before all else, who are kings!"

❧

The little gray I'm stroking reminds me of another little gray, Modestine, who accompanied the Scottish writer Robert Louis Stevenson across this same Auvergne countryside in the autumn of 1878. Beyond the horizon, toward the southwest, beyond Le Puy-en-Velay, Stevenson wandered across "a fine, busy, breathing, rustic landscape." "For twelve days," he recounts in *Travels with a Donkey in the Cévennes*, "we had been fast companions." The twenty-seven-year-old vagabond scribe had yet to pen *Treasure Island*—he'd do that five years later. But already he knew that each of us is a traveler in the wilderness of the world, each of us is somehow a traveler with a donkey. "The best that we find in our travels," Stevenson said, "is an honest friend." In Modestine, for 120 miles, from Le Monastier to Saint-Jean-du-Gard, Stevenson found an honest friend. "In this world of imperfections," he wrote, "we gladly welcome even partial intimacies." Stevenson embarked upon his trip after Fanny Osbourne returned to her husband in California. Sleeping *à la belle étoile*—roughly under the stars—while Modestine ate her black bread, he drank ice-cold water, tippled brandy, and meditated on his lost love. He arrived at his destination spiritually refreshed and healthily restored, ready to reclaim his lost Fanny across the ocean ...

It's hard to square the sound of braying against Schubert's piano sonata, his number 20 in A Major. Who could believe the tonality of such a duet? It's a slow melodic pitch punctuated by a deep, guttural plea—the sound of a lazy Sunday afternoon overlaid with an acute, stabbing pain. It's the sound of Balthazar lying down to die in a mountain meadow. Balthazar was the donkey in a 1966 film directed by Robert Bresson. Bresson uses Schubert's music to evoke a vision, a vision of a saintly mistreated donkey, bleeding to death from a gunshot wound. It's a tragic moment, our tragedy, says Bresson, who thought

7

the donkey "the most important, the most sensitive, the most intelligent, the most thoughtful, the most suffering of animals."

And he made a movie to prove it, *Au Hasard Balthazar*, with an unlikely lead: the expressionless Balthazar, the silent witness of human folly, the silent witness of a probing question: is it not human beings who make themselves look ridiculous through thoughtless cruelty and ordinary selfishness, through petty pride and mindless stupidity? Bresson said he wanted to create an animal pure of all falsification, wanted to tell "the life of a donkey with the same stages as a human's": the gaiety of the birth, the joy of growing up, the necessity of work, the mystical phase preceding death, and, finally, the tragic, moving end itself. Bresson's affinity is very much with the injured and the insulted of our world, with outcasts and sufferers. For him, the donkey is the pure sufferer, the ragged outcast. In creating something pure, Bresson more vividly highlighted how sullied we actually were. Beaten, whipped, and mistreated by successive owners, Balthazar's goodness arises from the fact that he never acts out of malice or spite. He brays and very occasionally kicks, but mostly he endures: his "dumbness" and "idiocy"—his passive wisdom—resembles Prince Myshkin's from Dostoevsky's *Idiot*, a text that inspired Bresson's filmic parable.

"I remember I was insufferably sad; I wanted to cry," explains Dostoevsky's epileptic Prince Myshkin. "I was finally roused from this gloomy state one evening on reaching Switzerland, and I was roused by the bray of a donkey in the marketplace. I was immensely struck with this donkey, and for some reason extraordinarily pleased with it, and suddenly everything seemed to clear up in my head." Myshkin's tale seemed comic to the young kids listening. They giggle as he admits he's "been awfully fond of donkeys ever since." Donkeys have "a special attraction for me," Myshkin says. "I understood at once what a useful creature it was—industrious, strong, patient, cheap, long-suffering. And so, through the donkey . . . my melancholy passed completely."

Like Myshkin's, the bray of Bresson's Balthazar is idiotic. But he's also ascetic and sublime, sensuous and holy, and he has a special window on our world. Balthazar is both a victim and a bearer of our truths—of birth and betrayal, of theft and cowardice, of sin and death. He doesn't say much. He simply suffers. The look in his calm dark eyes says it all: he understands. At the movie's climax, with a bullet wound in his thigh, bleeding on an Alpine meadow as Schubert's sonata plays, sheep surround Balthazar. They seem to know what's happening. He seems content to pass away among them. It's a tremendously affecting valedictory scene. You can't help but be stirred, feel sorrow over the donkey's tragic fate, a fate inseparable from ours. I remember being stunned after seeing Bresson's donkey fable. And I've somehow been touched ever since.

I'm freewheeling now, back on my bike, not going too fast, journeying down the other side of the valley. Over the hill is where I live, in a stone cottage, in a hamlet with seven other denizens. It's a far stretch for a working-class kid from Liverpool who'd always dreamed of living in New York. It's hard to believe I once set foot in the countryside only under duress. Ancient terraces surround me. They had vines on them over a century ago, lots of vines; a *phylloxera* epidemic devastated this vibrant local wine industry; then, between 1914 and 1918, a World War annihilated a whole generation of *vignerons*. Now sheep graze on the terraces, alongside the odd goat; only a handful of enthusiasts conserve traditional *cépage*. I can't stop thinking about donkeys, about that donkey LOOK, that donkey FEEL. I hear the wind whooshing in my ears, cooling my body, accompanied by Schubert and by the sound of braying. Everywhere around me are extinct volcanoes, the green upon green of the Massif Central's undulating moonscape; yet suddenly the beaches of Blackpool flood my brain. I'm drifting in late afternoon, riding not a bike but a ragged turtledove gray, for threepence, along the shore of a dingy English town.

He's ambling along, swaying as he shifts across the sand. I feel the saddle rocking from side to side, sliding under me, and hear the rattle of stirrups. And the smell, it's very vivid, the smell of dung, of discreet dung, of donkey odor, with just a hint of bran and barley. And of cotton candy, wafting over from the seafront promenade. It's the smell of graft, a kind of honest smell, a donkey-on-the-beach smell. For a kid like me, it's the smell of freedom, of remembering you're on vacation, of forgetting stuff, of childlike bliss. When I was young I always associated donkeys with the beach, not with the countryside; I associated them with water and sand, with wet sand, on account of the rain. It always seemed to rain then; if I wasn't riding a donkey, I played cards in the trailer, watched its windows steam up, listened to the downpour hit the roof. My dad would wipe away the condensation. Recently, I read that the two hundred donkeys waddling along Blackpool's beaches, carrying kids day in, day out for $4 a ride, had won a lunch break, an hour-long siesta, granted by the Blackpool city council, breaking up a shift that stretches from 10 in the morning till 7 at night. Donkey vets now also check hooves, ears, teeth, and coats, ensuring they're in tip-top condition. And owners whose animals don't pass the annual inspection won't be given a license to operate. I'm comforted knowing old acquaintances are being looked after, aren't being overworked for pleasure, for petty gain.

I'm almost home. The sun is setting. Soon be dark. There's hardly any traffic around here, biking toward Lavoûte-Chilhac, far from Blackpool, far from New York, far from anything I once knew with certainty, far from anything I ever imagined. I'm sailing downhill, rounding hairpins, racing without even trying, letting myself go to gravity. The sky has turned bright pink; craggy black silhouettes frame the horizon. I'm thinking about donkey patience and humility, about donkey exploitation, about stoicism under blows, about peace. I'm thinking about how I'm looking forward to understanding donkeys better, and maybe understanding the world and myself better, too. I'm looking forward to walking and talking, to walking and talking with a donkey, to stepping down from my bike, to leaving it behind propped up against an old stone wall. I'm looking forward to making a new friend in the wilderness of the world.

2

I WAS AWAKENED this morning by a turtledove. A good omen: the bird of love. Its magic flute, its song of songs, pipes from a tree somewhere not far from my ear. The time of singing has come, and the voice of the turtledove is heard in our land. Òcoo-OOH, Ooo-Ooo-OooÓ. In French, they're called *tourterelle triste*, and *triste* means sad. But this bird isn't sad, isn't in mourning this morning: she's content. The sun is flooding through the window and even at this early hour it's *hot*. I think of Gribouille, my frizzy-fronted partner, a big chocolate-colored donkey with a white muzzle and a red halter, my *compagnon de route*, whom I checked late last night in his little meadow, making sure he had some water and wasn't too lonesome out under the trees, in the mountain twilight. I could see the white specks around his eyes standing out like two half-moons in a starless night.

I inspected his hooves, looked underneath at his heels, at his soles and "frogs," the V-shaped sections around which pebbles and dirt can gather. A gentle tug on a donkey's lower legs is usually sufficient for him to show you the bottom of his feet. Frogs feel like rubber. I cleaned them out with a metal hoof pick, resting Gribouille's leg on my thigh, on flat ground, so he could balance himself. If he feels unbalanced, he'll never raise his foot. Pebbles irritate a donkey on a long trek, so you need to be attentive. I made up my packsaddle last night, too, with all I need for the voyage; simple things, things that won't overburden Gribouille. He's a strong lad—*costaud*, the French would say—and could bear 150 pounds on his back without any trouble; I've probably got about forty: three flannel shirts; a sweater for an evening chill; a Swiss army knife; a change of cotton pants and shorts; three pairs of walking socks; a toothbrush and toothpaste; deodorant and sun cream; a little rug for sitting on outdoors; a towel, two rolls of toilet paper, and three bottles of water; several well-thumbed books and a notebook. Oh, yes, and a bag full of stale baguette—*du pain dur*—broken into little pieces, for the odd treat and occasional incentive.

We're moving out of town slowly, along a narrow street with a couple of defunct cafés and a boarded-up baker's store, long gone. We pace the old cobbled street in a gentle, rhythmic, donkey tap dance. It's not a noise that jars, that startles or threatens, not a bullying noise of a fast machine; it's a hushed clip-clopping that reverberates off shuttered buildings with a kind of medieval melancholy, a melancholy of slowness, a soothing melancholy of hours whiled away. Overhead, crowning a steep butte, is a huge, yet ruined, stone portal from the twelfth century; it once led up to a fairyland chateau, reduced to ashes by a fire in 1698. This immense passageway is Allègre's crowning crumbling glory, a town whose name translates from its original Latin as "ardent and courageous." The portal wills me to enter into the cloudless azure, but I see a volcanic destiny ahead, a terrestrial force, over and beyond Mont Bar, soon to envelop us, to spread out around us. The undulations quiver in the morning haze like giant blobs on the horizon, giant blobs of ancient congealed lava. I'm a vagabond with a donkey, headed somewhere both holy and profane, holding the reins of another era, perhaps one to come, waving at passersby, saying *bonjour*, smiling, waiting for palm branches but mindful of speeding cars.

I'm walking alongside Gribouille with a slack rope, slightly in front of his drooping head. It's hard to say how long we've been walking. We're both feeling the heat, the sun beating down without much shade. We're headed toward a forest and we'll stop soon. Gribouille's natural instinct is to pull against any pressure exerted on his head by the lead rope. He pulls when he's seen something he wants to eat. He browses with his muzzle and darts toward anything that takes his fancy. He'll lurch with quite a force. He loves dandelions and thistles and bramble, everything that stings. He munches through them like he's eating a juicy apple. Afterward, he trundles along wistfully with half a field dangling from his mouth.

He and I learn to respond to pressure, learn together, to him pulling and me reining him in a little, to Gribouille knowing what I'm asking him to do, me understanding what he's up to. But we can't stop *all the time* for him to eat. So we develop a rapport, a mutual understanding. I pull gently and he responds; as soon as he responds, as soon as he moves along, I release the pressure. He knows we need to keep walking. If he doesn't respond, if he's *really* intent on feeding, on crunching yet another dandelion, his favorite roadside snack, I let him eat. I don't have much choice in the matter! Pulling won't work. The French have an expression: *un âne se pousse et ne se tire pas!* A donkey pushes himself; he's not pulled. After he's ripped up a few dandelion leaves, a firm tug usually gets him moving again. This is how we go. Walking and eating in unison, walking and talking side by side, one man and his donkey, on the move somewhere, slowly yet assuredly, along a rural yellow brick road. I rest my hand on his *poll,* the bony bump between his ears, a little lump that's a kind of gearshift, a secret lid. All around the poll is delightfully soft, the softest material known to man.

To stop Gribouille, I begin to pace even slower so he knows I'm coming to halt. *Attends!* When I stop, I calmly stand still, upright, with shoulders well back. I've a tendency to slouch in daily life, to feel the weight of the world on my shoulders, so this is good practice. I relax, breathe in, and exhale, listening to birds and the bees. Everything empties out. I slow down. Your body language needs to slow down with a donkey. You need to move like you're walking through waist-deep water, with steady, not jerky, movements. A careful, slower body language reassures a donkey, lets him gain confidence in you: small, slow steps toward trust.

The air is warm but fresh, oh so fresh, and dry: there's not a drop of humidity. It's quite high up around here, well over 3,500 feet. I breathe in again, and then exhale. I feel free and alive like I've never felt before. I relax and let the rope slacken, let everything slacken. Gribouille stops and for a magical instant we stand, absolutely stationary, next to each other, looking ahead, each lost in our thoughts, in our respective reveries. I can hear his deep, intermittent breathing, his almost sad sighing. He stares out into donkey nirvana; sometimes he'll stop on his own accord, seemingly without reason, just to listen and look, to take stock of it all. His head is frozen and absolutely calm. I watch in wonderment, watch a daydreaming beast go elsewhere, regretting my own profane clumsiness. It's not a dead empty moment, this, no mere pause when a donkey stops and nothing happens. I sense some profound *presence*, a fullness. Something *is* happening, something you can't see. "The essential is invisible to the eyes," the fox had reminded Saint-Exupéry's Petit Prince. A donkey concurs with the fox. Gribouille sighs, and then sighs again, twirls around his ears, dilates his nostrils, and slouches onward a moment later, apparently all the wiser.

❦

A promise always kept: the spring breeze. It returned after winter, along with the birds. Donkeys have burst out of their confines, brayed for absolute joy at their release, at their first sight of a new year's freedom, running into a wild greenness and mild air. Their coats are very shaggy and will molt as the weather warms. I'm combing Gribouille. He's the donkey who doodles, who scribbles freely on a page. Gribouille derives from the French word *gribouillage*, which means doodle or scribble, the noun from the verb *gribouiller*, to draw roughly. Gribouille equally implies somebody a bit simple, a bit naïve, maybe even a bit of an *idiot*, a lad after my own heart . . . I'm grooming him with a plastic currycomb in sight of a mighty stone portal, grooming the matted hair of a French donkey under a blue French sky, in soft spring sunshine, in a deserted field far, far away.

I'd quit an island metropolis off the coast of a giant continent and ended up—somehow—with a few donkeys on a tiny inland prairie. Since my tenth year I'd dreamed about going to America, to New York. I even had a big idea about living in the Empire State Building after that first trip in 1970. I'd gone there with my parents, who'd saved up for ages, forsaken a lot to make it over, to cross the Atlantic to see my mother's sister. She'd emigrated there a few years earlier. All my school friends couldn't believe I was going to America. For a long while afterward I had kept the free Pan Am shoulder bag we'd received on board the plane, and in it I stashed away my floor plan of the mighty man-made structure, then the planet's tallest. Atop of the world I saw before me my own destiny, down there, amid an endless yellow phantasmagoria, a flow of cabs, people, and possibility. Everything felt very strange for a *gamin* whose farthest voyage had hitherto been to a crummy beach in North Wales, where it rained all the time. Alien smells, funny names, heat, different colors, and litter, swirling mounds of litter being tossed around in the breeze. On every street corner I saw people doing nothing, just standing about, watching. I was captivated, vowed I'd be back some day.

The vow never went away; the dream persisted, even as I grew up, even as I should've known better. New York never left me, no matter where I went in adulthood. It was at the millennium when I finally realized this vow. I was back, for good I thought, forever, just before my fortieth birthday, living in a studio apartment not far from Central Park. My green card said I was now a *permanent* resident. For a few years I loved my Upper West Side neighborhood. I'd take strolls in the park, feed the squirrels nuts I'd bought at Mani's food store; I'd walk up and down Broadway, frequent Zabar's, watch the world go by on a bench across the street, along a thin, central slither of shrubbery called Broadway Mall; and I'd linger near the junction of Ninety-sixth Street, a little patch where Isaac Bashevis Singer fed his pigeons and where I could see my own *Shadows on the Hudson*.

Yet I never reconciled that New York dream. It was always too much to bear, particularly after it came true, and especially after it started to turn sour, turned into a high-maintenance monster that swallowed me up and spat me out. And all so I could spend endless lost hours in line at Duane Reade, with other lost people. As a kid I was dazzled by the Big Apple's magic, by its box of tricks; as an adult I saw only its sleight-of-hand, its trickery. Perhaps the vow had worn too thin. Perhaps it was too late. Perhaps I should've guarded it as a pipe dream.

☙

If I didn't comb hard enough, or in the right spot on Gribouille's *poil*, on his dark fur coat, I remember he knocked me with his muzzle, showed me where I needed to comb. He was talking to me with his head, his big brown head. It weighs a lot, and he loved it when I took its strain and supported it on my shoulders. Our heads were so close together then that I could almost see out of his eyes. After a while, he'd release himself and give me another prod, knocking me again, because, sometimes, he wanted to knock me; he'd thrust his head into my belly, give me a gentle knowing dig, a little harmless butt. His facial expression revealed nothing: it remained absolutely hermetic. His eyes were like two dark truffles buried in a deep hairy undergrowth. Hard to see into them, to sniff them out. If you tried to enter them, you'd lose yourself in an intimate immensity...

When I lived in another region of France, before I came to the Auvergne, I knew a brown mongrel called Gribouille. He was the baker's dog, the dog of a country baker who made loaves the traditional *Savoyard* way, in a wood-burning oven; Gribouille sat outside a store that was little more than an old workshop, an *atelier*. He would bark at everyone who came by. But it was a friendly bark, a bark of excitement. Nobody was ever menaced. I was always excited to see Gribouille, and he me. He did this strange thing: he'd put his jaw around your wrist, as if he wanted to bite you, and you'd stand there with your arm in his mouth. His teeth would leave faint traces.

Inexplicably, he'd never, ever break your skin. He did it playfully, and with incomparable skill. He followed me everywhere. We'd walk miles together, trek merrily across open meadows and muddy fields, and afterward I had to return him by car. One day, he waited patiently, even though I had to dig the car out of a pile of snow. He watched because he looked forward to his ride. He hopped into the backseat and loved to sit upright, panting, taking everything in like royalty with a chauffeur. When I left the region, I was too sad to say *adieu* to my friend Gribouille. And then I met another Gribouille, his kindred spirit who doodles with his muzzle, who's with me now on another trip, toward another future, through another door opening out to chance . . .

That first encounter with the donkey Gribouille had been surprisingly dramatic—and ecstatic. A herd of donkeys had hurtled toward us, joyful, triumphant, and running—they can really run! And braying at the top of their voices! But it wasn't me they were braying at. Rather, it was Jean, their owner, a jovial, bearded man in his mid-fifties, intellectual-looking in small wire-rimmed glasses and flyaway hair. Jean spoke passionately, inspiringly, about donkeys, about creatures he so dearly loves. He and I had driven a mile or so out of Allègre's medieval center and stopped at an empty field, or what I thought was an empty field. Not for long. No sooner had he parked his car than the sound of braying rang out across the meadow, from behind the bushes. Then the headlong rush: they'd somehow known Jean was coming even before he'd arrived.

Jean has been rearing and renting out his donkeys, and organizing donkey tours—*randonnées avec un âne*—for well over a decade now, ever since he and his wife Anne-Marie began their shoestring, labor-of-love asinine enterprise "*Âne-en-Auvergne*"—"Donkey in the Auvergne." He himself was smitten years back, he informed me, when he was all set to go off on a walking tour around France. He was a carpenter then, working in Geneva, but damaged his back in an accident, so couldn't carry a heavy knapsack. Somebody told him to get a donkey to bear the weight. He did; and that was that, and here we are with a drove of donkeys all pushing up against the fence, eager for food, jockeying for scratches. There must have been ten of them, of varying shapes and sizes and breeds. Some were bolder than others. Jean handed them stale bread and indicated their names: Victor, Jean-Luc, Pierre, Judie, Picotin ... oh, and yes, Gribouille, a chocolate-brown, the big, docile chocolate-brown.

Voici the doodler, the donkey I'd wanted to take with me, the donkey I thought I could rely on, could trust. It all happened a bit instinctively. He was the one. Jean told me he was a middle-aged donkey, a strong fellow who could walk long distances and carry hefty bags. Jean said he usually rents out his little *ânesses*, his little female donkeys, to families with kids; kids usually don't walk too far and sometimes get intimidated by larger males like Gribouille. Yet Gribouille was the most placid donkey you could ever imagine, with a drooping hound-dog look, the pure essence of tranquil melancholy. He was so gentle during our initial meeting; he seemed to me the nemesis of a world gone awry, a world I'd already decided to shun. He was just the companion I needed to flee with. A Chinese poet from the eighth century once spoke of how he'd encountered a traveler on the road, a traveler about to depart on a long voyage: "I dismounted and offered this traveler the wine of farewell. I asked him what was the aim of his journey. He answered me: I haven't succeeded in worldly affairs; I am returning to the Nan-Chan mountains to seek my repose there." What did this traveler search? "No noise," he said, "no confusion: all I want is a life pillowed high in emerald mist."

❧

Gribouille and I talk together sometimes, high in the mountains, in the emerald mist. We exchange words here and there, on the move, a traveler communing with his donkey. We've so far had some memorable conversations. He's brilliant at helping my French tongue. I'm hopelessly ungifted with languages. No natural talent. Never learned French at high school; in fact, leaving at age sixteen, I never learned *anything* at high school. A quarter of a century later, each Saturday, for years, almost without fail, I'd take the number 2 subway from Ninety-sixth Street up to Harlem, to 125th Street. I'd go to a tiny one-room apartment on 122nd Street to learn French from Victor, an out-of-work filmmaker, a French Breton, who hardly made ends meet. In a dimly lit Harlem room, I'd rote-learn conjugations. Then I'd walk home across Morningside Park, up its steep once-majestic tatty steps, the other side of St. John the Divine, the massive cathedral on Amsterdam Avenue, repeating aloud what I'd just learned. In winter, especially at dusk, outdoor revision in the park could be menacing. In summer, squirrels would leap out from the bushes while kids dunked basketballs in threadbare courts.

I've another French tutor now. Gribouille is patient and considerate, never interrupts, and always lets you finish what you want to say. He gives you time to pause, to reflect, to search in your head for the best word, for the mot juste, and then lets you enunciate it clearly and carefully. He looks at me as I speak and twirls his ears. He does it to be rid of the flies; but I know he's listening. I speak better in his company. I don't feel the need to rush it out, to hurry a phrase, to spit it out garbled or clipped. With a donkey, you speak *correctement*. If only every human encounter was like that! No matter what language. I'm all ears, too, little human ears, for his wisdom, and for his needs. He seems to instill patience in me, someone who's not always the best listener.

He brays sometimes, especially in the morning, and shows his big yellow pearls—his mighty incisors. At the start of each day, I rub his fringe and groom him with the currycomb, removing all the dust and grime from his previous evening's roll in the earth, the roll of liberty once the packsaddle and halter are off. He likes it best when I give him a good firm brush. It's a special moment together out in the field, before the sun is really up, when the ground is dewy and the air crisp. Then we saddle up for the day, and we walk and talk. More often, we actually amble along in each other's company in silence, lost in our own thoughts. Sometimes words say too much, Gribouille; they are the source of misunderstanding, of emptiness. Sometimes they're just blah, cellular hot air. Better to listen to the birds and the buzzing insects, to the crickets, hidden and in hiding, to the song of natural silence so difficult to find in our age of bits and bytes and clamor of facile technology. Listen to the crystal mountain forest, Gribouille. Listen.

Already we're inseparable, like Sancho Panza and Dapple, an ego and alter ego coursing through a dreamy tree-lined unconscious. Everybody remembers Don Quixote, the chivalrous knight-errant, astride his old steed Rocinante, journeying across Medieval Castilian plains, jousting windmills, searching for justice, righting the follies of a mad world, a world we know to be our own; but what about the simple, honest Sancho and his simple, honest donkey Dapple? There's lyric poetry and natural beauty in Sancho and Dapple's tender humility, a loyalty in which neither man nor donkey makes any demands, in which there are no manifestos or grand schemes. Instead, there's just an earthy togetherness and mutual caring, a love.

That's probably why Franz Kafka said Sancho was a freer man than his master Don Quixote, who had a "pre-ordained object" and was bound to the metaphysical duty of knight-errantry. But "Sancho," Kafka said, "harmed nobody"; and Dapple, his gray, bore the weight of his "swag belly," of Sancho's unrefined peasant habits, and did it without fuss or pretense. Like us, Gribouille, they weren't so much thoroughbreds as modest grafters, simple folk in search of simplicity, constant companions in good fortune and bad. They can't bear to part, not even for a moment.

When Sancho and the Don embark on the "Famous Adventure of the Enchanted Boat," leaving Dapple and

Rocinante secured to a willow tree beside the bank, "seeing himself about two fathoms from the shore, Sancho began to tremble in apprehension of perishing; but nothing gave him more pain than hearing Dapple raise his voice." "Now, Dapple," says Sancho to his master Don Quixote, "brays for grief at our departure ... Farewell, my dearly beloved friend, peace be with you, and may the madness that parts us be converted and undeceived, that we may be restored to your agreeable company." Sancho begins to weep terribly.

I like remembering lesser-known scenes from *Don Quixote*, ones that involve the squire and his Dapple; they're among the loveliest lines ever written about man-donkey relations, done some four hundred years ago by Miguel de Cervantes, the bulk of which he wrote in prison. "Oh!" sobs Sancho, after he and Dapple had plunged down a deep, dark pit, "what unexpected accidents, which, at every turn, befall those who live in this miserable world!" Sancho fears nobody will find them in their subterranean dungeon, that both man and gray donkey will perish as one, seep together into the sad earth of misfortune. "O, my dear companion, and my friend!" Sancho moans, until the Don finally comes to their rescue. "How ill have I rewarded thy good services? Forgive me, honest Dapple."

And then when Dapple goes missing, stolen by the dastardly Ginés de Pasamonte, the renegade robber and thief, Sancho is beside himself like never before, "uttering the most woeful lamentation that ever was heard." When he's eventually reunited with Dapple, the knight-errant's squire can't hold back his joy, nor his tears: "Sancho, running up to his donkey, embraced it with great affection, saying, 'How hast thou been, my dear Dapple, my trusty companion and joy of my eyes!' Then he kissed and caressed him; while Dapple very peaceably received these demonstrations of love and kindness, without answering one word."

3

WE'RE MEANDERING MIDMORNING. We started out early again because today will be long and hot—and uphill, climbing high. The weathermen have confirmed that it's another *canicule,* another heat wave here in France. It's steep trekking for a while, on a narrow stony path, traversing a clearing between two dense pine forests; there's a sheer drop into the valley. Trees are everywhere, stacked side by side. Giant spikes pointing upward toward the heavens. Tiny lime-colored lizards dart in and out of the cracks in the stone. I can see little specks of orange below, rooftops of a distant hamlet, a cluster of old stone houses, stones coming from these same mountains.

Gribouille moves elegantly and meticulously, placing his hooves down on the loose rocks, testing his footing out before he advances a single step. His caution is instinctive. He picks a route to avoid the stones, the rough ground. It's obvious stones aren't to his fancy. He always makes toward the very edge of a stony path, to the softer, greener earth. It's fascinating watching him in action as he shifts dramatically toward the margins; or, if there's greenery in the middle, he's there like a mighty brown shot. With his head drooping down and muzzle trawling the earth, it's as if he smells his way forth, nosing out his own personal passageway. It's said that donkeys can't see all colors, that they don't see reds; but they can certainly spot green. As he ascends, I hear the saddlebag scraping against the overhanging foliage and bracken. Closer to the edges means he's closer to what he wants to gobble; and he takes big, crunching swipes at what's in front of him. We walk together for a while and not much happens in the stillness. I hear him devouring half the local shrubbery.

The lead rope is slack because we both know what's needed to make this climb. There's no other possibility but up, over, and down. I let Gribouille stop; he eats again and I stare across the valley, looking out at the greenness. All kinds of things come to mind, cleansed thoughts, clear visions, uncluttered reflections. Space and time to ruminate. Nobody is in your face. Gribouille is happy feeding; me, I'm content following the horizon, flying over the trees. Then I give him two little pats on his neck, or on his rump. *Allez-hop!* And we're off again. We keep abreast. He's deep in pensive donkey thoughts, discreet thoughts, never really shared with anybody. Odd times I follow from behind, watching him tiptoe up the mountain unguided, saddlebags drooping to either side, tail moving in swishing simplicity.

When I first went walking with a donkey in Morocco's Atlas Mountains, I remember clutching my treasured

Basque walking stick, crowned with its wooden mushroom. I bought the walking stick in the French Pyrenees, years ago, from a lone makeshift roadside stand, from a beret-clad old man who sold *Ossau Iraty* ewe's-milk cheese. His three hundred sheep grazed out on the meadows, and he sold walking sticks to the odd passerby who emerged from the mountain mist and felt inclined to stop. But I soon learned that holding a walking stick *and* a donkey is a handful. It's too cumbersome; and people with batons bother some donkeys. They wince, thinking them cudgels or goads.

So this time I left my stick at home. Now, with my left hand, I hold the lead rope; with my right, from Gribouille's left side, his "near side," I feel the warmth of his poll and the strength and solidity of his neck. "We have to enter a donkey's way of doing things," I remember an English donkey-behavior expert telling me in preparation for this voyage. "We have to try to think with the donkey's brain, not with a human brain." What he said was sound advice: "Donkeys can teach us that physical force is insufficient: force doesn't work with a donkey. You can't *make* a donkey walk faster; you can't do things any faster with a donkey. We have to learn to go at its pace."

I tug the lead rope gently but firmly and we move along, upward. Robert Louis Stevenson, the peripatetic Scottish scribe, had thought differently. He wanted to go slow but not *that* slow. Like an inexperienced *ânier*, he lost his patience, tried to tug and thwack when tugging and thwacking doesn't work with a donkey. He piled Modestine up with a 200-pounds bundle, a giant mass on top of

a poor mousy-mite's back. He didn't really respect his diminutive beast of burden, didn't understand her curious
donkey ways. He didn't *try* to understand her curious donkey ways.

"Your donkey is very old?" a green-coated peasant
had asked Stevenson, watching Modestine advancing
slowly and pitifully along a lane.

"I told him, I believed not.
Then, he supposed, we had come far.
I told him, we had but newly left Monastier."

The peasant laughed, and, picking up a thicket, lashed
out at the little gray, lacing her across her moon-silver
rump. She utters a cry. "You must have no pity with
these animals," says he, setting an unfortunate example
for Stevenson. "Such a beast as that feels nothing; it is in
the proverb—*dur comme un âne* [tough like a donkey];
you might beat her insensible with a cudgel, and yet you
would arrive nowhere." A goad is the only thing that
works. Soon, upon leaving a village, Modestine's heart is
set on a byroad. Stevenson thinks otherwise. He loses
his temper and "strikes the poor sinner twice across the
face. It was pitiful to see her lift up her head with shut
eyes, as if waiting for another blow. I came very near to
crying." He realizes he needs to stop, wait, regain his
patience—that he needs to lighten the heavy load by
ditching stuff. Still, by ditching stuff, he says, "I now
had an arm free to thrash Modestine, and cruelly I chastised her."

Stevenson named one chapter of his *Travels in the Cévennes* "I Have a Goad." A goad—a spiked stick—does a pretty good job at goading, at inciting and urging, at tormenting somebody into doing something, be it a person or animal. "Blessed be the man who invented the goad!" proclaimed Stevenson. "This plain wand, with an eighth of an inch of pin, was indeed a scepter when put in my hands. Thenceforward Modestine was my slave. A prick, and she passed the most inviting stable door. A prick, and she broke forth into a gallant little trotlet that devoured the miles. It was not a remarkable speed, when all was said; and we took four hours to cover ten miles at the best of it. But what a heavenly change since yesterday! No more wielding of the ugly cudgel; no more flailing with an aching arm; no more broadsword exercise, but a discreet and gentlemanly fence. And what although now and then a drop of blood should appear on Modestine's mouse-colored rump?"

If I was walking this uphill trail alone, without Gribouille, I'd likely pace at twice the speed, perhaps even faster. But what would be the point of that, and to whom would I talk then? With a donkey, I'm compelled to go at their pace, to enter into their way of doing things. It's stop-and-go all the while. That's how it is with a donkey. I have to learn patience, to quell my impatience and frustration, my desire to hurtle along, to overtake, to beep my horn, to tear around the bend, to curse any dawdler who blocks my path. I'm no longer on a New York sidewalk, pushing past, nor in a car stressed out to nowhere, on a freeway that's come to a halt. Things work differently with a donkey on a dirt trail: patience becomes a day-dream that gently rocks from side to side, like a baby's cradle, or like a sailboat out on a windless sea. It's the gift of relishing the rhythm of precise steps, of treading slower yet going farther, of treasuring the present moment, making it endure longer, stretching it out in all its glorious fullness . . .

4

GRIBOUILLE SUDDENLY HALTS again, stops dead in his tracks. He's off staring out over the valley. I wait. It's weird where you drift, what enters an empty head full of blue sky. I'd learned a lot about donkeys from that trip to England, stuff Stevenson should've learned. I remember looking out to sea, at a sparkling blue-green millpond, at the English Channel in a rare May stillness. I was striding along Salcombe Hill cliffs, onward to Salcombe Regis, through grazing sheep and cows and fields that ran right up to the cliff edge, that tilted toward the sun, and that plunged into the sea, into Lyme Bay. I turned eastward and, through ash and sycamore trees, past stray pheasants, I headed toward donkey paradise. It felt like a majestic alpine meadow at sea level, in Devon, England. I was entering an otherworldly enclave beyond the banality of ordinary life, outside the bastions of human cruelty and carelessness.

Braying boomed out across the Kingdom of Donkey. I can hear it in the quiet of my mind's ear now. Perhaps Gribouille can also hear it. There's a bray now, and another . . . and another, this time a full call. It's an incredible salutation. Each bray signals the beginning of a perfect world. It's a bestial elegy to a windless dawn. It's the wild roar of innocence. I'm visiting donkey experts at Sidmouth Donkey Sanctuary, one of Britain's largest and most successful charities, full of Gribouille's cousins, cousins of all sizes and colors and breeds: geriatric cousins, blind cousins, neglected cousins, mistreated cousins, cousins whose feet badly needed trimming by a farrier, cousins who have been rescued from almost-dire fates, from the brink of death.

Sometimes a few patients are lost; but others have been reclaimed by the Sanctuary, nursed back to health, fostered out to caring homes, given a new lease on life, thousands of them. Still more live out their days in sunny Sidmouth, frequently well into their forties, very occasionally into their fifties. I'm here at the Sanctuary to talk donkey with those who know. Donkey smells creep up my nostrils. I feel a gentle tap from behind, a curious habitué who's out to make a new acquaintance, out to see what's what here today. I tell him I'm waiting, waiting to see Ben Hart, a donkey behavioralist, whose training unit is at nearby Paccombe Farm, who'll help me understand what goes on inside the donkey brain, inside your curious head-butting mind, inside Gribouille's sacred reposing stare.

"Donkeys are good at being donkeys," Ben Hart tells me, as we sit around a wooden picnic table drinking tea.

I *think* I know what he means. Ben has had a lot of experience working with equines. Before arriving at the Sidmouth Donkey Sanctuary, he spent time studying at the Californian ranch of famous guru Monty Roberts, "the man who listens to horses." "You *tell* a horse," Ben says, "but you need to *ask* a donkey." "If you're riding a horse," he explains, "and you approach a puddle or a stream, all you have to do is give your horse a little tap for him to gallop through; you *tell* him to go, *urge* him to giddy-up, and he moves. This doesn't work with a donkey. A donkey likely won't budge.

"With a donkey, you'll have to *ask* him to go through the puddle, you'll have to show him how deep that puddle is, show him how he can walk through it without danger." A donkey knows plenty of things, but "he's wary of things he hasn't seen before, things he doesn't know about. A donkey isn't good at solving problems that are *acceptable* to humans." "Our problem," Ben says, citing the *Talmud*, "is that 'we don't see things as they are; we see them as *we* are.'" So, I wonder, does a donkey's innate sense of self-preservation suggest stubbornness or stupidity? Or is it a different sort of intelligence? Ben Hart is emphatic: "A donkey's nature isn't to be stubborn or difficult, but purely to learn and survive."

It could have been then that *The French Lieutenant's Woman*, John Fowles's masterpiece Victorian novel from the 1960s, had entered my head; I'd been reading it during that Sidmouth trip, trying to imbibe the Lyme Bay atmosphere, "that largest bite from the underside of England's outstretched south-western leg," just like Stevenson helped me imbibe the Auvergne. What Fowles said about Sarah, the outcast eponymous heroine, seemed strangely apt for explaining donkey behavior: "Sarah *was* intelligent, but her real intelligence belonged to a rare kind; one that would certainly pass undetected in any of our modern tests of faculty. It was not in the least analytical or problem solving, and it is no doubt symptomatic that the one subject that had cost her agonies to master was mathematics. It was rather an uncanny ability to classify other people's worth: to understand them, in the fullest sense of that word." I remembered Sarah giving her own take on matters, on what we might construe as *donkey matters:* "What you call my obstinacy is my only succor."

"Donkeys have been domesticated for between five and eight thousand years," Ben continues, "and their ancestors have been evolving for sixty million years." Learning is crucial in this evolutionary process: if you don't learn how to adapt to different environments, he says, if you can't avoid predators, flee danger and external threat, it would've been impossible to survive so long. By that criterion, donkeys have fared rather well, suggesting a smartness not always acknowledged. "Donkeys learn things that are closest to their natural behavior and instincts," Ben points out. "Stuff that's completely unnatural for a donkey, like being driven, ridden, holding up their feet for the farrier, or traveling in a truck and box can take longer to learn because they're so far removed from their natural behavior."

But learn them, donkeys have. A confident, bold donkey—a donkey that's likely been well treated—isn't usually afraid of experimental behavior. He can pick up new stuff fast; a nervous donkey, fearful of the results of its behavior, may, on the other hand, have been badly treated and is trickier to teach. That requires a lot of patience. The most inquisitive and bravest donkeys tend to interact with their environment more frequently. They explore different options, reach different outcomes, and hence learn more readily: how to undo stable bolts, how to tip up water buckets, how to receive treats. Clever stuff! "A donkey's confidence level," Ben says, "affects his ability to learn."

"Can an old donkey learn news tricks?" I ask. "Of course," Ben answers. "Once you begin to stimulate a donkey mentally and give it problems to solve and challenges to undertake, it begins to learn new activities more rapidly." He gives an example of one donkey: "Cocoa came to the Training Center when he was about seventeen years old and has learned thirteen new activities that have helped to mentally stimulate him and deal with his problem behaviors, such as retrieve an object, bow, and carry a bucket. The more he learned, the faster he became at learning, and the more he wanted to learn. It took Cocoa a total of just thirty-seven minutes to roll out a carpet on command.

"Donkeys are motivated most successfully by things they find naturally enjoyable," Ben says. "Food or scratches, social interaction with other animals, or being released into a grassy field. Not all donkeys are motivated by the same things, or motivated at the same level. The use of scratches to motivate is reminiscent of two donkeys grooming one another—and it's been scientifically shown in horses that grooming can lower the heart rate of the animal." Ben reckons that "shaping" the behavior of a donkey is most effectively done through "Positive Reinforcement," through "anything that, occurring in conjunction with an act, tends to increase the probability that the act will occur again." Positive Reinforcement is anything a donkey will actively work for, anything that encourages him to continue to work for reward.

Ben shows me what is meant by Positive Reinforcement, "the kindest and safest and most effective way to teach and change behavior in a donkey." Soon we're in the courtyard of Paccombe Farm Training Unit, with a nervous little silver donkey—Wilson—and his trainer Liz. He's a lovable little fellow, and timid, timid. Liz wants to lead Wilson under a rope full of brightly colored flags of yellow, red, green, and blue. The rope is placed six feet above the ground and stretched between two poles ten feet apart. This is a whole new experience for Wilson: he's not sure about any of it. How to get him to pass underneath? Show him it doesn't hurt, show him there's no danger, speak to him but not with words. Suddenly, another donkey in the compound, Dusty, a confident one, walks blithely under the regalia as if it's child's play; yet it's lost on Wilson. He's demure and keeps his head down in quiet desperation.

Liz urges Wilson to take a step nearer the banners, leading him gently by adding pressure to a slack rope. He moves ever so closer: she rewards him with a tiny ginger cookie. Once in a while a little cookie doesn't harm a donkey. No dialogue is exchanged between Liz and Wilson: they interact exclusively through body language, through gestures. Liz tries the same maneuver again, urging another gentle, tentative step. Wilson obliges; she quickly offers him another little cookie. (She has to do this within a short time frame, at the most several seconds, otherwise Wilson won't be able to associate what he's just done with the reward he receives.) Liz repeats the cookie routine another time after another step, and then another step and another cookie ... and another and another ... It's painstakingly slow, yet quietly meditative to watch. They stop for rest. Wilson looks a bit more reassured. Liz has the patience of a saint. She ignores all unwanted behavior: only *wanted* behavior is rewarded.

Liz knows food can create bad habits, like spoiled and demanding behavior, because food is sometimes used as a bribe. We tend to give donkeys food treats without thinking about the consequences and behavior we're encouraging. If we repeatedly take a morsel of food out of our pocket, and the donkey spots us doing so, he'll soon begin to poke around himself, shoving his warm snout into our affairs, "mugging" us for another treat. When we reprimand him for drooling over our coat, the donkey gets confused. We encouraged this behavior, yet suddenly changed the rules without giving him time to figure out why. He's told off ... but for what? He might then try to snatch a few crumbs, inadvertently biting someone. Again, it's a problem we've created, not one the donkey has, who's behaving consistently, who's doing what's he's already been shown to do. All of which doesn't mean we can't give a donkey a little treat; it means we must be mindful about how and why we do it, and how often.

In Wilson's case, he begins to associate a forward step with something *positive*, with being rewarded a little cookie. He's learning to take just one small step, a little like Neil Armstrong on the moon surface, doing it for mankind. He slowly associates the trainer and a forward step with a positive situation, with a reward that occurs *during* and *because of* certain behavior. He's using his brain to make the correlation. Importantly, food is being put to good use because it's given *only as a reward* (i.e., after the event), *not as an incentive* (i.e., a bribe before the event). Wilson never actually made it under the banners, under the rope—not that day, anyway. But after an hour or so of Positive Reinforcement, he's very close. Tomorrow, Liz will try to go all the way; and once it's done a single time, Wilson will know that it's safe to do again, perhaps even to repeat by himself.

Positive Reinforcement—patience and little rewards, tender acts of kindness and encouragement—is worlds removed from a mentality that wants to punish, that wants to dictate behavior through violence, through goading. We see it every day in the news. Punishment is a more developed, pathological form of "Negative Reinforcement," defined as anything that a donkey will *avoid*: pressure from the bit (the mouthpiece), jerking the lead rope, threatening eye contact, noise, pushing from behind on the rump, being struck . . . We know too well those classic bundling images of somebody trying to push a donkey, or tugging them into doing something they don't understand or are uncertain about. We push and pull and tug and get hot and bothered and then stop, believing the donkey knows what we're demanding, and resume pushing and pulling and getting hot and bothered again, only to find the donkey more resistant than ever.

A donkey won't know it's doing anything wrong, because it's not being shown what's right. And the more he's reprimanded for getting it wrong, the more Negative Reinforcement spills over into punishment, into blows and pain, into loud noises and violence, into poor handling and misunderstanding; the donkey will dig in its heels and be even more unresponsive. So it goes. But punishment never changes the fact that undesirable behavior has *already taken place*. Any punishment, too, would have to occur three seconds or less *immediately after* the perceived misdeed, otherwise a donkey won't associate what they've done with the punishment dished out. More likely, punishment will have the animal shun a person or situation they associate with the punishment.

If punishment "succeeds," it succeeds only as a short-term fix. The donkey won't learn anything, nor will any human. And a donkey will doubtless repeat the behavior that initially prompted the punishment. Indeed, in all likelihood the punishment will lead only to more punishment: a mild rap here anticipates a more severe whack there. Escalating anger and frustration on the part of the owner or trainer coincides with increasingly aggressive postures toward the donkey. Meanwhile, the donkey gets nervous, is frightened to take decisions, becomes stubborn, maybe even aggressive himself. It's a lose-lose situation, like warring nations. Dialogue breaks down, mutual distrust reigns, animosity becomes the order of the day. Thus, concludes Ben Hart, Sidmouth's resident expert: "Punishment is ineffective and resented by both donkeys and humans. The consequences are dangerous and damaging to the donkey-human partnership." "We might also remember," Ben tells me upon parting, "that our own state of mind and emotional condition affects our donkey's behavior."

5

YOU NEVER KNOW what you're going to encounter en route. I don't miss a thing. I touch everything, feel things, smell smells I've never smelled before, not smelled since long ago. Reality opens out with clarity, pierces my senses. I'm discovering lost worlds of rural antiquity and hidden pleasures of the self. I follow little yellow markings— *balisages*—painted on tree trunks, on gates, on stones underfoot, on telegraph poles, on crumbling walls, heading down trails that lead across moors and mountains, streams and ditches, bridges and brooks, meadows and prairie, to little human settlements, sometimes only two or three stone houses. Properties are often falling down, abandoned by people who could no longer live off the land; others are poor yet prim with vital pride, breathing an earthy peace, a lost-world languidness. Simple wooden shutters and neat flower boxes, roaming livestock—hens and rabbits, sheep and cows, dogs and cats, horses and donkeys, yes, donkeys, who bray at Gribouille, touch his nose, sniff him, and stare into his deep, deep eyes.

Villages just about survive, like hardy plants on far-away islands. We enter and leave them like a pair of castaway botanists in summertime. Things go slow, slower than walking pace. An old peasant woman, thin and wizened, ventures over to us and smiles at my *beau* beast, strokes his front, asks me from where I've come, and where I'm headed. It's a familiar question. Not far in actual distance, I say. What's this lad's name? Monsieur Doddler. Is he very old? Quite old. He's been around the block a few times. A few gray hairs on his soft brow. Her teeth are rotten, her hands callused, lined with hard labor. In French, *labourer* means to plow the land, to till. We exchange pleasantries under a blinding Auvergne sun. Then she's gone . . .

Hours pass, perhaps days. You reach the point sometimes when something has got to change, when something has got to give, when the world everybody revels in seems all wrong to you, when it's hard for you to function in it anymore. You feel *under*whelmed, disappointed by what's there, feel the need to step back, to take a look at yourself, at where you are, where you're headed, at what's wrong, at what's not working here. This is a very hard thing to do: escaping before it's too late. I was struck one night watching a DVD—*My Dinner with André*—one hot sultry night in New York when the A/C is cranked up, watching a film made in the early 1980s. It was a strange film, without much happening. No action, no music, no gimmicks or stars: just a quiet, theatrical set piece. Perhaps that's why it struck me.

Two men, old friends, who haven't seen each other for a while, meet, share a meal at a New York restaurant, perhaps on the Upper East Side, and talk about what they've been doing. One man, André, once a celebrated playwright, talks a lot, about his mad mystical capers in deserted Polish forests and in Tibet and India, about him fleeing the limelight; the other, Wally, also a playwright, a struggling one, a skeptic, listens with an incredulous ear. The dialogue starts off lightly, whimsically, but then its intensity and gravity gets ratcheted up. Imagine, says André, imagine you're in a play, having to improvise, but in this case, *"you're* the character, so you have no imaginary situation to hide behind, and you have no other person to hide behind. What you're doing, in fact, is asking those questions that the actor should constantly ask himself as a character—Who am I? Why am I here? Where do I come from? And Where am I going?— but instead of applying them to a role, you apply them to yourself."

There it was, applied to myself: Who am I? Why am I here? Where do I come from? And where am I going? It was as if it had been me around for dinner that night, as if Andy was having dinner with André. I was teaching for a living back then, but didn't want to teach because I had nothing more to teach. Instead I wanted to learn, wanted out, wanted to change myself, to explore something new ... I didn't know what. So I got out, made a run for it. And here I am, walking very slowly, flourishing in the silence, beyond the frantic din. Where I'm headed I don't really care, because I'm present again, whole, truly alive, connected. Gribouille stares at me, curiously, somehow knowingly, with deep mournful eyes, nodding, shaking away the flies. We keep walking, hearing voices in the field, voices inside my head. The poor beast is listening, listening to my thoughts, just listening, without answering one word.

He's listening. He tiptoes onward, his ears slice through the hot air. I accompany him obediently, watchfully. Great masses of dark leafiness surround us: millions of skinny conifers, huge clumps of ancient oaks and big beech, with dense undergrowth, secret lairs for insects and little mammals, for spores and lichen, for worms and ferns, for nocturnal beasts in deep slumber. An ornithological whistle plays a complexly orchestrated mountain chamber music. It doesn't awaken the sleeping.

There's nothing on my mind, yet somehow I have total recall. We've arrived at a little brook at the bottom of another slope, and another lost hamlet that hugs the incline, with rumpled stone buildings and bright terracotta roofs; trademark curved *génoise* tiling, neat waves of ornate cornices decorate the guttering. The brook flows in a gentle, soothing white noise. A dog races over to greet us, barking menacingly, but stops at the boundary of his own territoriality. Neither man nor donkey crosses that threshold. He's harmless. He yaps to break the boredom and doesn't bother us. But you have to watch out, be careful of unknown dogs with donkeys. They can upset one another. I pat Gribouille and he pricks up his ears and appears unbothered. Nothing seems to bother Gribouille. I rub his face, just above his nostrils, and feel his damp breath, an animal warmth on my hand. He snorts, trembles, and seems about to bray; but the inclination passes.

6

WE STOP UNDER an old oak tree. We made it over the top of another great hill, and we're down the other side now, on lower undulating ground, in the valley, awaiting the next descent. I've secured Gribouille's rope around the tree. I've replaced the short lead rope with a longer one, with *une longue longe*, and fastened it with a quick-release knot. The packsaddle is off, and he's happy munching grass. I'm about to unpack my little feast. I'm sitting on my rug, about to eat. I've found a little corner of the world in which to dine in peace. It's no longer easy to do; there aren't many quiet corners left.

I'd much rather lunch alone on a piece of bread, said Sancho somewhere in *Don Quixote*, "without all your niceties and ceremonies, than eat turkey at another man's table, where I'm obliged to chew softly, to drink sparingly, and to wipe my mouth every minute." I love this. A baguette, bought this morning, which I break into pieces, stuffing some in my mouth. I lean over to give Gribouille a morsel of very stale baguette, breaking up the hard loaf with my hands. He takes it skillfully from my flattened palm. With a Swiss Army knife, I slice off a chunk of cheese for myself, *brebis* from the Cantal, sheep's cheese from a neighboring *département,* which is sweating and softening in the heat . . .

There used to be heaviness once, an iron in my soul, long ago. It bashed open my skull. I watched my adolescence dissipate into damp Liverpool air. I remember the sordid miasma of old insane times. I'd walk along a road beside dockland, a desolate trek to the shipping company office beyond the city center. There, aged sixteen, I filled out forms while somebody stole my youth. A merciless walk, a bleak journey even in the height of summer; I began the job in the depths of winter. I had to pass a grain refinery that spewed out crap, millions of tiny yellow pellets that stank. They'd stick to your face, cake in your hair, seep into your skin. I sat behind a desk, sifted through paper, through bills of lading, through import and export forms, stamped them and passed them on to somebody else. There was idle chatter. Phones rang. People breezed past, came and went. They didn't say much.

I've spent half a lifetime trying to turn back the clocks, trying to rediscover a paradise lost. I felt long ago that the grown-up world isn't all it's cracked up to be, that I had to invent my own truths to get by, that the realm of possibility lay elsewhere, somewhere I had to invent, off-road. Years later, a lifetime later, I've retired to a cottage faraway from anywhere. Amid its deep song silence, I scribble a few harmless lines and commune with loyal, silent friends who stand by me in thick and thin, who've never let me down, who're beside me now; I accept their braying counsel when I vowed to listen to nobody. They've offered an understanding ear—two understanding ears. These days my adventures are more clandestine, daydreaming fantasies rather than wide-awake facts, Northwest Passages of the imagination, dramatized by lost innocence, of dealing with a world that offers little of what I want.

I suppose I've always had idiotic dreams, weird fantasies, at least since I read Dostoevsky's *The Idiot,* or perhaps his *Notes from Underground.* It might have been because we were both clerks—he, the underground man, had been a clerk, a petty clerk in the Russian civil service. That could have been the basis of our initial bonding, of our strange friendship. He was a man alone, a man who inhabited a "mouse-hole," a wretched apartment in a tenement block in St. Petersburg, over a century ago; he was more than twice my age when I'd discovered him, around forty years old, Dostoevsky said, "living like this for a long time, for twenty years or so." "I was a nasty official," his underground man claimed. "I was rude and enjoyed being rude. Why, since I took no bribes, I had to make up for it somehow."

We hit it off immediately, Dostoevsky and I, despite our epochal differences, despite our different tongues. I was nasty and rude back then, and I enjoyed being nasty and rude. It was all I could do, of course, for not taking bribes, for not wanting in. I was serving my time, paying my penance, as a wages clerk at the dock board, after getting fired from my old job at another dock board, the one near that grain refinery. A man called Frank sat opposite me, chain-smoking and masticating. Frank entered numbers on forms that had boxes, lots of boxes. He was about sixty and my immediate boss, showing me the ropes that steadily tightened around my neck.

I plotted revenge on Frank, revenge for Frank simply being Frank, revenge like the underground man sought with the army officer on the Nevsky Prospekt. I needed to vent rancor on somebody, or on something, to let people know I existed. Frank rode his bike to work every day. He propped it up in a storeroom nearby. I'd disappear from my desk for long stretches; I'd meditate on the toilet, think about being elsewhere, stare at the door in front of me. Afterward, I went to the storeroom and tampered with Frank's bike, letting the air out of his tires, bending a few spokes here and there, wrenching the steering, loosening the seat, all of which was joyously satisfying, a spiteful beastly pleasure.

I saw myself, perhaps fancifully, perhaps realistically, I don't know, as downtrodden, as an outcast, with ideas and ideals I'd forever foolishly endorse, *stubbornly* pursue, no matter what anybody said. I wanted to be thrown out the tavern window in a brawl, as the underground man had, in order to *feel more alive*. At first, Frank didn't suspect anything untoward. Eventually, he got suspicious. They all got suspicious. There were limited culprits. These incidents hadn't happened before. I was a new recruit; it was a new occurrence. It was pretty obvious. What did it matter, anyway? I wanted them to find out. My conduct was poor. Nobody liked me; I didn't even like myself . . .

I wasn't always like that. I was forced to grow up, compelled to be defensive and nasty. Kicking out didn't come naturally. I'd always been sensitive, a nice kid, who once cried terribly because of his dead pet mole. Maybe I never really recovered; it was the first time I'd seen death—the death of my little fluffy mole who I'd found on the roadside. We'd been traveling back from walking in the hills of North Wales, my dad and I. We were near a place called Loggerheads, a real place, driving along a quiet back road when all of a sudden we encountered this mole in the middle of the road. He was distressed, seemingly injured, oddly above ground. He'd lost his way somehow, and I should've let him be. But instead I picked him up; he was still warm and very soft and he had these funny pink padded feet with tiny fingers, which felt even softer than his fur; and this pink wet nose and I could see his dark beady eyes poking out, dazzled by the light, all crinkled up. He was terrified, I think. So I took him home, carried him back to the car, cradling him, really wanting to care for him. I was afraid a passing vehicle might strike him.

When we arrived home, I put him in a cardboard box, filled it with rolled-up newspaper, and spread pieces of white sliced bread for him to munch on, not knowing these mammals eat only insects and worms, loads of them, up to fifty pounds' worth each year. I thought he'd be warm and safe in the box, and I left it overnight in the garden shed. Every once in a while I went back to peek if he was okay. He'd stopped moving, had nowhere to move. The next morning he was dead, very dead indeed, in the box, sort of solidified. His little padded feet were pointing upward as if he was trying to burrow his way out, flee into the garden. I guess he'd eaten too much bread. We buried him in the earth, returned him to where he belonged. For weeks and weeks I cried every time I thought about this poor mole, who'd done no wrong, who'd fallen afoul of the human world. And it was me who killed him, the little wounded creature, finished him off for good. I was so upset. I still think about him forty years on, as other moles tunnel in our garden, pile up soil on the lawn. It was my initiation into softness, into a softness that perishes ...

The taste of the cheese reminds me of the Pyrenees, and my walking stick, and the old man at the roadside. I went back again, Gribouille, years later, and you know what, he was still there, always there, probably still there as we speak, in the exact same spot, exact same man, selling his cheese. The *brebis* is on the bread and I enjoy a simple everyday pleasure, no frills necessary, just like Sancho. But I smell pure Auvergne, not Pyrenees. There's a fragrance here that doesn't carry elsewhere, that's unique, a sweet odor, of chamomile mixed with wild lemon thyme. I cut a thin slice from my dried sausage, duck sausage—*saucisse de canard*—heavily seasoned and very garlicky. I've a mini saltcellar, too, and sprinkle a few grains onto some radishes. Life is sweet. Cheese and sausage, some fresh air, a few radishes. I swig water from a plastic bottle. I'll refill it in the next village, swill my hands clean of the grease, let Gribouille lap from the fountain if he wants.

I chomp away and look out over a sloping meadow. The shaded warmth on my bare torso is agreeable. I watch Gribouille's muzzle poking around and hear his loud crunching. Cows graze, beautiful *Limousine* cows, with shining ochre coats. There's a battalion of trees behind them, in perfect formation, evenly following the hill down to the roadside. A field of maize is nearby. The landscape flows like a tapestry stitched together from random bits of green and yellow cloth. Suddenly, above me, branches start to shake and rustle about. Perhaps it's a light breeze, much needed; maybe it's a red squirrel up there, dancing around, a little red imp. I saw one yesterday spring out in front of me; when the sunlight caught him he looked glowing orange with a blazing bushy tail. I can see a pack of swallows push back theirs, streamlining themselves to dive-bomb through the sky, playing with each other in their blue backyard, flying with such rapidity that it's hard to track them.

It's sleepier down here at ground level, the domain of vagabonds and loafers paying their dues in a medieval rite of passage, circa Second Millennium. The flies bother Gribouille. He keeps trying to shake them off. Every once in a while he stamps down one of his hooves, making a curious thumping noise on the earth. His tail is swishing. Both are signs of a discomfort I put down to the temperature, though maybe he's missing his pals in Allègre. I pat his head and rub his coat along his back and loins, over his head and legs, checking for sores and bugs and lumps. Nothing. I scratch his withers and knock away the flies from around his eyes. I clean out a little discharge that's built up there. His ears prick up as I speak, as I ask him if *tout va bien*? The whole countryside is aglow in burning golden silence.

Perhaps back then, in my office-boy days, I saw myself as a bit of a donkey, a donkey who gave the occasional kick, letting it go as a kind of revenge, harboring a grudge like the donkey from Alphonse Daudet's short tale "The Pope's Donkey," who'd saved up its kick for seven years. This donkey served the Pope for years and years when there were still Popes in Provence, in Avignon. The Pope loved his sure-footed she-donkey, rode her everywhere. She was as gentle as an angel, esteemed by all Avignon. But one day a young rogue had the idea to enter the Pope's service, to make good his stead. To impress the Pope, the rogue began feigning kindness on the donkey. The Pope fell for it, but the donkey recognized the rogue's deceit.

In secret, the rogue pulled the donkey's ears, tugged her tail, drank the papal wine she loved to drink. As a practical joke, the rogue led the donkey up to the bell tower one afternoon, all the way to the top, and left her there stranded, in full view of everybody below, claiming she'd clambered up on her own accord. The townsfolk had to haul her down. People then lost a little respect for the donkey; so did the Pope. The unhappy donkey didn't sleep a wink afterward, and plotted revenge. Yet soon the rogue is made a lord, profiting from the finagling, and is sent to the court of Naples. He doesn't return for seven years, comes back to Avignon for a big ceremony. All the assembly is present, and the Pope greets them, with his donkey at the foot of the steps. The rogue approaches her smiling, patting her on the back, making sure the Pope is watching. Then the donkey positions herself. "Here you are! Take this! I've been saving it up for seven years now!" And she launches an awesome kick, so awesome that the smoke and dust from it could be seen far off, with a feather whirling around: all that was left of the rogue himself . . .

Kicks from donkeys, says Daudet in his tale, aren't usually that emphatic or dramatic. When a donkey is faced with a problem, with an unexpected change of environment, or feels threatened, he can kick. If a donkey is nervous or doesn't trust a handler, she'll want to escape. If they can't escape, if they're confined to a small space, tied up or held by a handler, they'll resort to kicking. Just like humans. For a donkey, kicking becomes a successful defense mechanism against things they feel threatened by. A donkey thinks kicking out works, so he'll try even harder next time, irrespective of whether the handler is nice or mean. But, as experts point out, donkeys prefer not to kick; they'll often offer threat-kicks, warning shots across the bows, a form of donkey communication telling people to watch it, or else. On the other hand, if donkeys are handled correctly, with patience and persistence, using Positive Reinforcement, and if their "comfort zones" are suitably expanded rather than threatened, even confirmed kickers, experts agree, will kick very little, will have no need to bear a grudge, will have no cause to meddle with somebody else's bike.

7

GRIBOUILLE IS EATING a thicket as I leaf through a book, a long-out-of-print 95-cent Signet Classic whose destiny is to be read in the open air, in the sun: *Platero and I*. Its cover is fire-red with a golden border and a picture of a sad, elegant man with black goatee and yellow chapeau, a dapper sun-tanned rider from Andalusia sitting upon his merry gray donkey, Platero. It looks like a child painted the image. "Is *Platero and I* a kids' book?" somebody once asked author Juan Ramón Jiménez, who won the Nobel Prize for Literature in 1956. No, he said, it isn't a work for children. "This short book, where joy and sadness are twins, like the ears of Platero, was written for . . . I have no idea for whom! . . . For whom lyric poets write . . ."

But Jiménez wrote *about* a donkey, a melancholy prose poem, "an Andalusian elegy" on the brink of war, in 1914, a donkey who was the very essence of goodness and peace, a small donkey, "so soft to touch that one would think he were all cotton candy, that he had no bones." "He is tender and loving as a little boy, as a little girl," says Jiménez; "but as strong and firm as stone." "He is made of steel," someone thinks. "There's steel in him. Both steel and quicksilver."

The spot where I'm sitting is so solitary that even turning the pages of *Platero and I* seems to condemn this idle shaded arbor. Poet and donkey wander through dawn fog and midday haze, through the moonlight and the starry heavens, through torrid summer heat, a torrid summer heat I can somehow feel. Platero nibbles at the sparse grass on shady walls, at the dust-covered squash and the yellow sorrel. "We understand each other very well," says Jiménez. "He is so like me, that I have come to believe that he dreams my very dreams."

Yet people wonder: Who is this man dressed in mourning with the quicksilver donkey? And what's he mourning?

The misfortunes of man, those unexpected accidents that Sancho said at every turn, befall us who live in this miserable world? Perhaps the poet is mourning the wonderment of nature, its eternal beauty, its splendid spectacle, so hard to endure, so easy to plunder? "Do you know, Platero, from where comes this sweet flora, this sweet flora I usually ignore, flora that daily casts a mantle of tenderness over the countryside, leaving it softly rose and white, or pale, pale blue?" Perhaps you know, too, Gribouille, who those two silhouettes are, those two who've been heading off into the ghostly distance, who've hovered over the mountains like a pair of dawdling clouds? Who could they be but us?

One of Jiménez's favorite words is *eternity*, the poetic moment that endures forever, that's untouched by the slightest impurity, that takes corporeal form in the hills and trees, in the moon and sun, in blossoming flowers and in little Platero, Jiménez's emotional landscape, his animal Other: "I stop in ecstasy before the twilight. Platero, his dark eyes scarlet from the sunset, walks off gently to a pool of rose and violet waters; he dips his mouth gently into the mirrors which seem to turn liquid at his touch . . . The evening stretches out beyond itself, and the hour, touched with eternity, is infinite, peaceful, beyond sounding . . ."

With exquisite charm, Jiménez lets Platero bray at Baruch Spinoza, our best-known philosopher of eternity, and bray at us. Only intense reflection and self-reflection, detaching itself from all life's clutter and clatter, says Spinoza, can discover the eternal. "We feel and know by experience," he wrote in *Ethics*, published posthumously in 1677, "that we are eternal." We feel and know ourselves not as little cogs in a shifting, facile world, but as eternal beings in a grander holistic universe. It's very hard to do, finding this state of mind, finding this state of peace, this freedom. "But all things excellent," Spinoza says, in the last line of his great work, "are as difficult as they are rare."

Jiménez found Spinozian peace of mind with his little donkey Platero. No matter where he went, Platero and eternal nature went with him, stayed in his head, endured as his poetic vision. Even when the poet fled Spain in 1936, after General Franco came to power, Jiménez still tasted pomegranate and honeysuckle, still heard braying and bells, still basked on dusty Andalusian hills. Even wandering around New York's concrete jungle, where Jiménez lived for a decade, teaching at Columbia University, even amid its bustling throng, its clanging concrete and steel, the sentimental poet dreamed of a natural world he could barely see, hardly perceive anymore; even then Jiménez preoccupied himself with imagined beauty: "The moon! Let's see! Look at it between those two tall buildings over there, above the river, over the red octave beneath, don't you see it? Wait, let's see! No . . . is it the moon or just an advertisement for the moon?" "Below the George Washington Bridge," he'd said, "the friendliest bridge in New York, runs the gilded countryside of my youth . . ."

And even after Platero's death, so tearful for any reader, so sad to see him stretched out on his bed of straw, his eyes soft and sad while the poet pats him a final time, the gray donkey lives on. "By noon Platero was dead. His little cotton belly had swollen up like a globe, and his discolored legs stuck stiffly skyward. His curly coat looked like the moth-eaten flax of an old doll's hair that falls at the touch in dusty sadness. Flying about the silent stall was a beautiful butterfly, its three colors shining each time it passed through the ray of sunlight from the little window." "Platero, it's true that you see us, isn't it? Yes, you see me. And I think I hear you, yes, yes, I hear your gentle, plaintive bray in the cloudless west, filling the valley of the vineyards with sweetness..."

8

I PICK UP on a songbird, warbling away, up there, and a distinctive crunching of grass, down here, next to me, where a brown donkey digs for buried treasure, munches his secret cache of mulch. The city is elsewhere, that past life, adolescence, kicking out... is drifting away, almost buried, an earlier chapter, read many times over, lived and worn out already. My comfort zone is expanding. Chamomile wafts through the forest, and pine, freshly cut pine, and beech, too, beech trees, slightly lighter coloring to their barks, smokier. We're moving off, descending a little, going toward another valley, through another forest. There are millions of forests around here, wild ones and managed ones, acres and acres of them, green mountains covered naturally with beech trees, forests rising to over 4,500 feet. In the shadowy obscurity, in the afternoon twilight, I see a crossroads ahead.

We approach it along a path carpeted with pinecones, and an entrance to a narrower, darker tunnel under a low leafy canopy. Mysterious blackness and mosquitoes. Gribouille stalls because he's not sure what's ahead, what's there in the half-light, along the passageway. I'm not sure either. I let the rope go free and walk ahead, entering the dim shaft, making sure he's watching me, ears pricked up, body erect. He won't budge an inch till he knows. I cross the menacing threshold, show him there's no concern here, nothing to fear. I walk back, reclaim the lead rope, give a gentle jolt, and he responds, convinced; together we move into the tunnel, into what has been slashed through the mossy undergrowth.

A forest is a place where the wind blows no more, where the birds refrain from singing, where the crickets hold their tongues. The feeling of emptiness in the middle of a living system, with its audible silence, causes a shudder, a fear, an inexplicable reticence. Gribouille has it; I have it. The earth below echoes with a hollowness as we step over it, eyes skinned, wondering what's in among the trees, what's hidden. Can we slip through the forest while avoiding the trees? Gribouille almost breaks into a trot; he's moving that fast. I'm really bounding to keep up. He wants out, out of the forest. He's headed toward an open clearing, searching for light, for sunshine, for what the existentialist philosopher Martin Heidegger called "the nearness of distance."

However, a problem soon besets us. Ahead, a massive tree blocks our path, has fallen down, probably in a storm; its trunk and branches are sprawled across our passage. We have to cross this barrier, or else turn back. There's no going around. Either side is a steep, pathless slope: only down or up; and down is a big, scary drop. The path slopes almost with the gradient. It's easy for me, with two legs, to step across, not too close to the edge; but, for Gribouille, with four legs, it's another story, a complicated task. Perhaps he's encountered the tree before? Perhaps he knows the track, knows a method for crossing over it?

He's stopped to survey everything, to assess the problem, discreetly and thoughtfully. I remember my donkey training from Sidmouth: if there's a problem, and if the donkey refuses to advance, there's always a reason: *often it's the donkey who will propose the solution.* He's not going to budge till he's ready. Let him be, let him figure it out himself. I can assist by removing the packsaddle and the *croisillon*—the wooden crosspiece support for each saddlebag—letting him move more freely, lightening the load he needs to carry across. Surreally, a group of walkers has appeared behind us, out of the forest depths, apparently from nowhere. Where did they come from? There are about ten of them, all dressed in fluorescent walking gear that looks very new and clean. I let them pass by. Yet they're interested in Gribouille: they want to stand by and watch what he'll do next.

My friend now has an audience as he pokes his muzzle into the trunk, sniffs it, and lifts up his dainty leg, sort of testing the water. He's too close to the edge, so he retreats, knows this crossing point isn't going to work. The trunk is thinner that end, but there's danger from the drop. So he pokes his nose higher up the trunk, away from the slope, and takes another step, a higher step. He's still not sure. He shifts back again. We're all watching, fascinated, gripped by a donkey intent on resolution. After a few moments of reflection, he finally goes for it, and with an elegant, precise high-step, one front leg passes over ... then the other ... and then a hind leg drags over ... and then a fourth leg, the second hind leg; he's there ... he's made it over the obstacle. Everybody starts to clap. I feel very proud, and give him an enthusiastic pat, a rub of encouragement. He's typically deadpan, typically expressionless. I saddle him up again, and we depart from the crowd, continue on our lonely passage, on our good companion solitude ...

♧

Martin Heidegger spent many a lonely hour in a simple wooden ski hut in his beloved Black Forest near Freiburg, Gribouille, where he was rector of the university. He could see the Alps out of the window of his nineteen-by-twenty-two-foot cabin. Here was Heidegger's "elemental world of Being," the quiet sustenance for his thinking, base camp for his comprehending the "hidden law" of the mountain forest. Heidegger saw the dark forest as a metaphor for life, for all reality. Truth tends to conceal itself in the forest undergrowth, he said, in the quietness, where some routes—"blind alleys," Heidegger labeled them—trail off and lead you nowhere. But others take you to the truth, to the open ground, to the clearing, if only our thinking can find this clearing, can find the right *feldweg*, the right forest way, a path known only to the local woodcutters, to the local lumbermen.

Heidegger pinpoints two types of thinking: *calculative* thinking, and *meditative* thinking. Calculative thinking, he says, "computes ever new, ever more promising and at the same time more economical possibilities." It never stops, never collects itself, races from one subject to the next. Meditative thinking is thinking that "contemplates the meaning which reigns in everything that is." The latter "is what we have in mind when we say that contemporary man is in flight-from-thinking." Of course, nobody profits from meditative thinking; critics say it has lost touch, that it finds itself floating above things, unaware of reality, beyond the "real world," that it's worthless in business, a waste of productive time; and time is money.

Yet meditative thinking doesn't just happen by whim. In fact, it demands greater effort than calculative thinking, which usually requires no effort at all and isn't hard to do. Meditative thinking, Heidegger says, needs as much delicate care as other genuine crafts. There's no instant gratification. It must be able to bide its time, wait like the farmer for the ripened seed, or the *bûcheron* who doesn't chop down all the trees, nor burn them all at once. He bides his time, as the *vigneron* lovingly guards his wine, storing his logs away, drying them, making ready for when it really gets cold.

Heidegger believes each of us can follow the path of meditative thinking; each of us, in our own manner, within our own limits, can find the woodcutter's path, can seek the clearing. "Why?" he asks. Why, "because man is a *thinking,* that is, *meditative* being." As such, there's nothing "high-flown" about meditative thinking, about turning down the sound, about tuning in to something more meaningful for a while. It's enough, he reckons, to dwell on what lies close up, to meditate on what concerns us, each of us, here and now; here, on this patch of ground; now, in our present moment of history.

Yet what's closest to hand is easy to miss, easy to overlook, and often hardest to grasp. Meditative thinking asks that we let ourselves go, engage in what "at first sight does not go together at all." So we ponder, we wait, we meditate on what's there, grope for openness, for a clearing, for light, an expanse in the distance, on the horizon somewhere. We see close up but we reach out toward this horizon. Meditative thinking draws us into the distance while we stay put, while we stay near. It brings these two realms together, is a sort of *nearness of distance*—a "coming-into-the-nearness of distance," Heidegger calls it. Finding the "nearness of distance" boils down to finding our path to *Being,* to full awareness, to releasing ourselves.

9

IT'S LATE AFTERNOON. We're passing through Bonneval, a picturesque village, neat and proper, atypically *Auvergnat.* Normally, in little villages rusty old farm devices and ancient plows, piled-up tires and tarpaulins, wood, assorted debris, and abandoned car chassis litter everywhere. Here there's none of that. Instead, I'm sitting on a low stone wall surrounded by beds of brightly colored flowers interspersed by little lawns of lush grass. The old church is opposite and there's a lovely *auberge* next door, a country inn with a shaded terrace overlooking the valley. Everything has been lovingly restored around here. It feels like a showcase Alpine village. It's somehow all in bloom on a bright summer's day. I attach Gribouille to a ring next to the fountain, which trickles water. He sticks his muzzle into the well but desists from drinking. The birds are chirping, and I stroll past the *Mairie*, the town hall, not much bigger than a family house, toward the inn for a coffee.

Suddenly a top window of the town hall opens. An elderly woman's head pops out. *Monsieur, Monsieur!!* It's me she's hailing. *Votre âne, votre âne! Il faut absolument qu'il ne mange pas les fleurs!* Your donkey! Your donkey! He must absolutely *not* eat the flowers! I tell her he'll never eat those flowers. Donkeys are very particular about what they eat and drink. He never eats domesticated flowers! He only eats wild varieties in the field. He doesn't like supermarket food! He prefers dandelions any day! She doesn't believe me. She *mis*trusts poor Gribouille! We know this chestnut: Tattered outlaw of the earth!

By the time I've returned with my coffee, to drink sitting on the wall, *Madame* is out there, ostensibly reading her book, on the bench next to the church. She can better survey us from there. Gribouille sniffs every flowerbed, shoves his nose into all of them, seems mesmerized by their coloration, by their odor . . . I'm not sure why; but he never, ever eats a single flower, not one, even though it *looks* like he does. Instead, he eats only what he wants: he devours the grass like the giant fluffy lawnmower he is. Yet by now the coffee tastes bitter and the village starts to feel oppressive, like an ornament; we're unwelcome, derided, outcasts, a team of spoilers. A short distance out of town, I look back and see *Madame* inspecting the flowerbeds for herself, she of little faith, and I think of Father Chichambre, the village priest from *Culotte the Donkey,* Henri Bosco's 1937 donkey classic, another kids' book for adults, who quietly warned: "And now, if you want to please your old pastor, who truly loves you, then when all is said and done, be nice to the donkey Culotte." Yes, be nice to the donkey Gribouille.

Culotte the donkey, like Robert Bresson's Balthazar, like my *camarade* Gribouille here: all take the brunt of human ridicule in their stride, humbly, as they amble from side to side, as they probe us discreetly with their deep, knowing eyes. With monstrous head and sickening cry, they're seemingly the devil's walking parody, not welcome in any neat village full of flowers. The donkey Culotte comes from sunny climes, from the lavender land of Provence in the south of France. Culotte is smart: He doesn't like the winter cold. So he wears "beautiful trousers of shiny, brown velvet corduroy, attached at his chest-strap and at his neck by suspenders of well-polished leather." Everybody laughed at poor old Culotte wearing *culottes,* for he cut a sight. Daily he suffered jeering yells, as well as the odd rap on his rump; but never did he let it show, never did he let it get to him, bowing his muzzle solemnly as he went, advancing with scrupulous little steps through the village's cobbled streets.

Culotte ran errands for a strange mountain hermit and became the source of poetic wonderment for a small boy, Constantin. Through Constantin, Bosco could keep hold of his own personal paradise, his childish sense of worldly awe. Bosco retreats into the *super*natural and everything seems more real, and more meaningful, than ever before. Culotte, we hear, was a donkey "who was no more out of place in the square in front of the church, than in his stable; a donkey endowed with a soul, good to the unfortunate, honoring his gods; a donkey who could pass everywhere with his head high, for he was honest; a donkey who, if there were rights among donkeys, might have been the glory of his race." It was said that something indefinably powerful and tender watched over Culotte: "Wherever he went, this occult benevolence accompanied him."

He was an unobtrusive donkey, was Culotte, a bit past his prime perhaps, like Gribouille, his gray coat well brushed, modest-eyed, without insolence or meanness, who knew he was a donkey and didn't blush at being one. Culotte knew how to walk, stop, start off again, turn around, drink, graze, look, listen, obey, just like a donkey. He was "a donkey that certainly loved reflection; a donkey that had seen much, retained much in his lifetime; a donkey that had pardoned much; an affectionate donkey, sensitive to good manners, polite in his contacts with donkeys and deferential without contempt in his relations with men; a donkey who could be presented anywhere."

Still, old Father Chichambre was right: people nonetheless lacked respect for Culotte. Everybody made fun of him, except the boy Constanin, who, like a lot of small children, is mesmerized by the donkey's benevolence. Constantin seeks the remarkable Culotte out, against his parents' will, following him into the magic kingdom up in the hills, where all life is harmonious and land fertile. Is this paradise a fantasy, a product of Constantin's fertile imagination? Or is Culotte's habitat real? And if it's real, is it just for kids? Are we mistrusting, incredulous adults good enough to enter it, ready to peek into its mysterious charm, cross its banished threshold?

"I heard stones rolling down the forbidden footpath," Bosco has Constantin muse. "And raising my head, I saw the donkey, emerging from among the oak trees, the famous donkey about whom I still knew nothing. He was no longer wearing his winter breeches, undoubtedly because of the unusual mildness of the air. With his head lowered as if to sniff the stones, and with careful hooves, he came down the steep lane. He passed, letting his little, light-donkey steps clatter on the flagstone bridge. The shopping baskets dangling from his back were filled to the brim." Culotte approached Constantin, came so near that he touched the boy. Then he spoke aloud, in a human voice: "Climb on my back. Do not be afraid. You can ride bareback, without a saddle. I want to show you the mountain ... I know you love the mountain ... Come! We will set out for the Highlands."

10

COME! LET'S SET out for the Highlands! Gribouille nods his muzzle, bashes me again as we depart, fleeing where we're not welcome, seemingly in agreement—though much likelier to ensure that I keep stroking the bit between his ears. And then we're off again, taking a narrow, stony path that descends quickly, going down toward a brook. It's a delightful passage under the trees beside the flowing water. We wander past a couple of lone cottages, summer homes for city slickers. I can tell by the cars, by the big clean cars, and their number plates. We rejoin a tarmac road and then walk and walk, journeying through other villages, grimier settlements, where people smile at us, welcome us. That's usually the case, more the rule: that passersby smile, often smile, when you're walking with a donkey.

There are a surprising number of people out and about in early evening. Everybody turns their heads to look at Gribouille, and then grin. Whole villages beam when we trundle through. People with donkeys attract attention that's different from horse riders or dog walkers.

And a lone hiker journeying through these parts would pass largely incognito, barely getting a second glance, let alone a cheery grin. Unlike a horse or dog, almost nobody fears a donkey, not even a little child. In fact, it's often little children who adore donkeys most, who'll wander up first, whose attention is gripped quickest. People of all ages want to stroke your companion, utter an amicable word, inquire about him or her, share their own donkey tales. There are few people who don't have a donkey tale to tell.

We clip-clop up a hill, between old, old buildings, the odd little workshop—there's one making traditional clogs—a café and a shop selling regional products. It's probably something about a donkey's placid look, their slumbering *lenteur*, their infectious slowness and drooping presence that grips peoples' attention, that brightens up your day, that creates softness and affection. It's the look of a pensive child, forehead pressed against the windowpane, like Constantin watching the rain outside, looking for Culotte. Who can resist the sad yearning to go out and play? Perhaps with a donkey, kids can see themselves looking out of the window, see their own damp reflection. Yet it's puzzling: the smiles donkeys stimulate set against the cruelty they sometimes suffer, the derision they incur, the silly stereotyping.

❧

Donkeys have long been on the receiving end of human pillory, long been one of our favored whipping beasts. You know better than anybody, Gribouille, the fate of long-lost cousins. In literary form, G. K. Chesterton's 1920 poem "Donkey" exemplifies such asinine fear and loathing, yet shows equally how donkeys often get the last laugh, always find their fill, like Homer says in the *Iliad*, when he compares them to the great warrior Ajax pelted with Trojan spears and blazing faggots: "in such discontent, Ajax withdrew before the Trojans, much against his will . . . Even so, he was as stubborn as a donkey who gets the better of the boys in charge of him, turns into a field they are passing, and helps himself to the standing crop. So many sticks have broken on his back that their feeble cudgeling leaves him unconcerned, till at last they drive him out with much ado, but not before he has eaten all he wants."

Chesterton, the English writer-poet cum philosopher-theologian, the witty creator of Father Brown whodunit yarns, seems ambivalent about donkeys. The vehemence he voices for three quarters of his first-person-donkey stanzas strikes the reader as genuine, maybe because *our* vehemence toward donkeys is genuine. When the accursed donkey took to the earth, Chesterton says, a society of dumb, ragged outcasts was thereafter in our midst.

> *When fishes flew and forests walked*
> *And figs grew upon thorn,*
> *Some moment when the moon was blood*
> *Then surely I was born*
>
> *With monstrous head and sickening cry*
> *And ears like errant wings,*

The devil's walking parody
On all four-footed things.

The tattered outlaw of the earth,
Of ancient crooked will;
Starve, scourge, deride me: I am dumb,
I keep my secret still.

And yet the much-maligned fugitive has his moment of glory, his sweet hour, and Chesterton brings himself around to acknowledge it:

Fools! For I also had my hour;
One far fierce hour and sweet:
There was a shout about my ears,
And palms before my feet.

Those palms before the donkey's feet were spread when the Bible wrote of Jesus riding into Jerusalem, on "Palm Sunday," on the first day of the last week of his life. "Go to the village opposite," said Matthew's gospel, "where you'll at once find a donkey tethered with her foal beside her; untie them, and bring them to me." A donkey had been chosen, fulfilling the Old Testament prophecy of Zechariah: "Rejoice! Here is your king, who comes to you in gentleness, riding on a donkey, riding on the foal of a beast of burden." Crowds of people carpeted the road with their cloaks and cut branches from palm trees, spreading them in Jesus' and his donkey's path. He'd chosen a sturdy, modest mount, an animal who'd take you somewhere, gently and safely; not a shining, proud, rapid steed, but an ordinary beast, a tortured creature, the bearer of a pacifist cause with a cross of his back, the *Croix de Saint André*.

Donkeys usually figure in a positive light in the Old and New Testaments, and in the Koran. They shine as loyal and intelligent creatures, as the bearers of wisdom, as trusty mounts of prophets, sometimes even cleverer than the prophets themselves. In the Bible, like in the Koran, donkeys are frequently called *asses*. But not in the popular, pejorative guise that associates ass with fool. The *Oxford English Dictionary* says that polite people use "donkey" euphemistically, should they want to avoid the cruder-sounding "ass." Cervantes has Sancho Panza explain that Dapple is how he wanted his donkey known, since Dapple, the apple of his eye, his gray, was no ass, only the loyal friend of a simple squire.

The root of the word "ass" is classical: *asinus* from the Latin. Since the ancient Greeks, who were as ambivalent about the donkey as they were about everything else, in fables and parables, the ass has come to exemplify clumsiness and stupidity. The phrase *asshead* dates from 1550, 44 years before Shakespeare had Bottom wear one in *A Midsummer Night's Dream,* turning the wandering, easygoing clown-weaver into a dumb nincompoop. *To make an ass of oneself* harks back to 1590. Ass as an idiom for "backside" hails from 1860, from nautical argot, and became common parlance in the 1930s. Initially the expression was "arse," a word still used in British English. The loss of the "r" in American English is traced to 1785, glimpsed in other uses, e.g. burst/bust, curse/cuss. *Asshole* first appeared in 1935.

Even though the Koran says "the ugliest voice is the ass's voice," donkeys verbalize insightfully with Muslim prophets—or, more accurately, Muhammad verbalizes with donkeys. Miracles in the Koran aren't so much that Allah enables animals to speak the language of man as that Allah permits Muhammad to speak the language of animals. Allah preserves a man, his food *and his ass* for one hundred years. "We shall bring forth a beast of the earth to speak unto them because mankind had not faith in our revelations." One "black, haggard donkey," Ya'foor, actually responded to Allah's questions, swore loyalty to the prophet, and eventually became Muhammad's right-hand donkey. Muhammad rode Ya'foor everywhere. After he'd dismount, at the prophet's behest Ya'foor would knock at peoples' doors with his muzzle; and when an owner came to answer, the donkey would signal, by nodding his head, that the prophet wanted him . . .

11

PERHAPS YOU KNOW, Gribouille, how we humans have all too often revealed ourselves as collective Judases? Stevenson, the enlightened wordsmith with a donkey, spoke about his "Last Supper" with Modestine, whom he was soon to betray, selling her off just as they'd finally developed a mutual affection, just as she was eating out of his hand in the moonlight. Perhaps you know, too, Balaam's parable, Gribouille, Balaam the prophet-for-hire from the Old Testament Book of Numbers? He betrayed and chastised his donkey, but, like in Bosco's *Culotte,* his donkey talks—or rather talks back—tells her master why she acts the way she does, confronts him about his cruelty, about his blindness; thus the Bible dispels chestnuts about any "dumb ass."

The only *asshead* around was Balaam; his donkey was the clever one: she awakened Balaam from his apostasy, from his conceit and search for pecuniary gain. In the parable, the humble donkey saw, was spiritually enlightened, and glimpsed the angel, while her master didn't. She acted apparently bizarrely, strangely, irrationally; and yet inside the donkey brain, by stubbornly wandering off the road, she acted rationally, intelligently, and faithfully. It was a faith soon betrayed. Balaam was corrupt and beat his companion, mistrusted her loyalty, saw dollars rather than good sense.

God told Balaam not to go with the Moabites and betray his people, and himself. Yet he's promised great honor and wealth—the "wages of unrighteousness"—so, unsurprisingly, Balaam succumbs and leaves. "Let nothing stand in the way of your coming. I will confer great honor upon you." He saddles up his donkey, departs next morning with the Moabite bigwigs, until an angel with a drawn sword blocks his path. The donkey sees the angel and turns off into a field. Balaam beats his donkey to bring her back on track. Then the angel "stood where the road ran through the hollow, with fenced vineyards on either side." Once again the donkey sees what's ahead, and, "crushing herself against the wall, crushed Balaam's foot against it, and he beat her again." Soon the angel moved on and blocked a narrow path where there was no room to turn either right or left. So the donkey lay down under Balaam. "At that Balaam lost his temper and beat his ass with his stick."

Henceforth the real action begins, the awful truth: "The Lord made the donkey speak, and she said to Balaam, 'What have I done? This is the third time you have beaten me.' Balaam answered the ass, 'You have been mocking me. If I had had a sword here, I should have killed you on the spot.'" Then his donkey asks, querying Balaam's trust, "Am I not still the ass which you have ridden all your life? Have I ever taken such a liberty with you before?" "No," replies Balaam, only for God to open his eyes, to make him see at last the angel with the drawn sword. The donkey is vindicated. Balaam bows his head solemnly, shamefully. The angel takes up his donkey's cause: "What do you mean by beating your ass three times like this? I came out to bar your way but you made straight for me, and three times your ass saw me and turned aside. If she had not turned aside, I should by now have killed you and spared her." Thus, "a speechless donkey," recalled the Gospels, "spoke with human voice, and restrained the prophet's madness."

I love the parable of Balaam's donkey because I can really imagine a donkey veering off the roadside, really imagine you, Gribouille, veering off the roadside, nudging your frizzy muzzle, flapping up your ears, steering your master out of harm's way. It all seems believable to me, as realism rather than religion: these actions are convincingly donkey, a model of undefiled donkeyhood. But Balaam doesn't see anything, doesn't know what's happening, and, like a lot of us, in his blindness he gets mad and impatient. He's been made a fool of, and *that* niggles him. So he needs to vent spleen somehow and chooses violence. In the end, it's he who's the fool, he who can't see the folly of his ways, who's blind to other kinds of insight.

❧

I'm standing behind Gribouille. Our day is over. I'm removing the packsaddle and his red halter. The first thing he always does is roll about in the earth. He's really going for it, and the dust flies everywhere around him; his legs curl up like a little child in a womb, and he wriggles and wriggles with innocent joy. I can see his underside, his white belly. Then he sits up, rests his body on all fours, and stares out dreamily across the valley. It's a magnificent vision. He's in a wonderful meadow for the night, open on all sides, fresh and calm, with Mont Bar looming in the distance. The location is aptly named: Bel Air, *fine air*. The stars are already twinkling. When I see him in this natural state, I rue burdening him each day with my load. After a while, he stands up again and looks a foot taller, revived and robust, with his ears upright like intergalactic antennae. I approach him with the currycomb, intent on giving him a really good grooming before bedtime.

If you stand behind a donkey, their ears look like angel wings, flapping in the breeze, two flexible handlebars you can grip for taking off, for floating upward toward the heavens, up there, beyond the mountains. Gribouille's ears are brown angel wings, with white shadings in the middle. He's blessed with his own built-in radar. At the rear is his tail. This not only swishes to shoo away the flies; it's a rudder that gives us stability, that keeps us on course through the great green ocean we're traversing. It's flailing about now, twitching in unison with his wings, tuning in to some distant divine frequency, like a conductor's baton leading a great symphony orchestra, or perhaps a metronome ticking to Schubert.

I can imagine Gribouille as Balaam's donkey, imagine him seeing angels, pointing them out to me with his muzzle, tapping me to ensure that I stay out of harm's way, that I don't get ideas above my station, that I don't get seduced by any sirens with luring songs. I hope I don't; I hope I don't have to tie myself to any mast. It's important that I take heed, not to betray his veering wisdom, don't become another Balaam-for-hire, another Judas, someone else who believes a donkey will eat the flowers. Gribouille turns back to look at me plaintively as I comb, twisting his neck, like the angel of history Walter Benjamin spoke about, the German philosopher who perished in 1940, who never quite made it over the mountaintop. I remember Benjamin being inspired by a little Paul Klee watercolor drawing called the *New Angel*, a spindly abstract figure with a pair of wings and eyes glancing slightly over its own shoulder. The angel's face is turned toward the past, says Benjamin, but he's also reaching out toward the future, toward somewhere ahead. "Where we perceive a chain of events," this angel, writes Benjamin, "sees one single catastrophe which keeps piling wreckage upon wreckage and hurls it in front of his feet."

The angel would like to linger to awaken our dead, to watch over us, to repair what's already been smashed, to clear away our debris. But there's no time, and perhaps it's too late anyway. He nods his head toward the future, toward paradise; and a breeze gathers and catches in the angel's wings, a storm that's going to propel the angel irresistibly toward this future, toward paradise. When I first read Walter Benjamin years ago, after returning to school, after a ten-year gap, a lost decade, I never thought the angel of history might be a donkey. I never thought Balaam's donkey—with open ears and head tilted backward, staring at me now like Culotte stared at Constantin—could help me understand the pile of debris Benjamin saw as accompanying the storm of progress.

12

THE SKY IS pale blue this morning and the stars still twinkle in the dawn light. A delicate mist haloes the meadow. Gribouille is slouching toward me, slouching toward Bel Air rather than Bethlehem, ambling from side to side, through the mist, ambling with what I conceive as a wry frown on his face. Whenever I see him ambling like this, apparently ambling for ambling's sake, tranquil in his thoughts, sufficient unto himself, all my worries, my past life, the world of growing up and growing old, everything that turned out to be much *less* than I'd anticipated on the eighty-sixth floor of the Empire State years and years ago . . . all of it floats away into the crisp morning air.

When I wandered around New York, prowling its streets and broad avenues most afternoons, afoot through shadowy passageways and cavernous subway stops, dreaming of Walt Whitman, searching for a song for myself, I never imagined I'd end up walking, let alone talking, with a chocolate-colored donkey along deserted French lanes and in open fields. I'd wanted to be as carefree as Whitman, an aimless New York loafer, marveling at its pageant, at its glorious jam, at its inventiveness; but its unfeeling isolation, its brutal indifference, left me cold, had me in panic about whether I could afford a future. Back then, with Walt, every day was a Saturday afternoon, open for business, rubbing shoulders with the world, with a world that was intent on spending, spending, spending; now, with a donkey, it's always Sunday, a slouching Sunday afternoon in which every second counts. Yet there's nothing to buy nor anything to sell, or any watches, only a donkey a little after dawn . . .

※

Gribouille isn't in the mood for walking today. He's dragging his feet a bit. We're going very, very slowly. Some days you get like that, don't you, days when you're not in the mood. A donkey is just the same, no different there. He's stopping a lot now, and not always to eat. He simply comes to a halt and that's that. He waits and watches: I wait and watch his gaze, wonder what's up, if anything. It's always a strangely serene moment. He breathes, sighs, and freezes. I'll never really know why. I don't think he's tired.

Perhaps it's the track, perhaps there's a problem with his footing? I get him to show me his feet. Nothing bothering, nothing gathered. The track is dusty red volcanic soil, dry and slippery and full of little loose rocks, millions of pieces of lava with blowholes, tiny, tiny bubbles. It's a narrow trek, steep again, and Gribouille definitely doesn't like this surface. That's the problem. I coax him on, lead him near the edges; I accept his pace, try to keep him moving along. Patience. A lot of patience. We work together for a while, my arm around his big head, staying tight to the margins of the track.

He's doing much better now as we near the summit. We're up and over and heading toward a forest. We're traveling on level ground, out in the open. The trail is softer underfoot, a lush fir carpeting. He's moving surprisingly briskly inside this arboreal living room. On odd occasions, he overtakes me, literally pulls me along. I follow. He can really zip along when he wants, only to suddenly stop again, reflecting upon the silence, face-to-face with a quiet world, a donkey in the midst, a man going deeper and deeper into the velvet hush. The sun shines through the gaps in the covering. I photosynthesize in nomadic liberty...

It hits you sometimes, just for a moment, when you enter a patch of sunlight: a feeling of being free, of realizing you can do what you want, go where you want, that you're answerable to nobody. Accept your donkey. For an instant, you almost smell it, feel its tingling force. Liberty. I'm the first man on Mars, the artist as a young man, the Consul drinking mescal, the King of Spain, penning my own diary of a madman. I'm a fraud, a charlatan . . . I'm stubborn, I'm honest, I'm shy, I'm arrogant . . . I'm a crook . . . I'm anything I want. And anybody. I'm even me, yes, plain old me, affirming my own self, a stiff from Liverpool with a brown French donkey. Who would've believed it! Not me. People change, can change, sometimes for the better.

❧

Hitherto, I'd lived my life sort of vicariously, modeled myself on somebody else, a character in a book, a famous writer, a famous professor; I read what they read, dressed how I saw them dressing, decorated my house as they decorated theirs. I'd been fiercely independent, yet I still sought guidance, needed nourishment from somewhere, wanted somebody to look up to, to admire. Maybe it was because I'd not found it at home, with my parents, who were kind and loving but not book-smart; or maybe, like a lot of younger people, like a lot of journeymen serving their time, I needed a mentor, a teacher figure, a crutch to prop me up until I'd learn to walk, solidly, on my own two feet—beside a donkey.

When I moved to New York, I chose the Upper West Side because I dreamed of the book-lined apartments I'd seen on West End Avenue. That set the tone of a life I thought I wanted to lead: a tenured professor, tall ceilings, a doorman, a public intellectual, a bagel for breakfast, riding the subway up to City College, with Hannah Arendt under my arm. I remember walking down Broadway late one Saturday evening, very late, in January, in a brutal cold; the wind ripped off any bare flesh. I wore ski gloves and my rabbit-skin cap, with its flaps turned down, covering my ears. I'd raced up forty blocks to the newsagent near 112th Street and found myself on the front of that week's *The Nation*.

I was delirious, drunk on pride, and floated down a deserted sidewalk, down another forty blocks, all the way back to Sixty-ninth Street. I'd written a review of a Walter Benjamin book, with his angels in Paris, and made the headlines! Henceforth I'd be famous, the talk of the town: West End Avenue, here I come. I'd realized an ambition— at least I thought I had. It'd taken me twenty years to dig myself out of the two-bit dock-board hole I was buried in, somehow succeeding where my old mole friend hadn't. A high school dropout had not only made it to New York; now, apparently, he was a New York intellectual, too. So I'd finally found what I'd wanted, what had been *obsessively* driving me on all those years. After a while, though—a very short while, in fact—I knew it wasn't what I wanted, recognized it wasn't really me. It was painful to admit, and I didn't admit it quickly. Of course I could have let it be, ignored things, carried on regardless, feigned the ruse of a false self, wrapped myself up in other people's clothes; but, as Shakespeare's Lear said out on the heath: "O, that way madness lies; let me shun that. No more of that."

What folly! Folly of wanting to be something I wasn't, of playing another game, not my own. New York had started to eat away my brains. It wasn't a good place for just being you. There's too much success dangled in front of you. It's hard to resist the game. And there aren't any donkeys either, only worn-out horses who tug buggies around Central Park. It was time to leave, even before I'd barely arrived. I was Balaam wanting to go straight and fast, emboldened by conceit, by ambition, by wealth, like Sancho being promised his island governorship. That ridiculous. I know it's banal to say that the *idea* of happiness, of someone else's, isn't the same as *real* happiness, as happiness that's lived out, practiced to the full. But it's true. Real happiness comes in unforeseen places, through surprising twists and turns, through honesty. The straight and narrow is usually a lie, a lie to oneself.

13

NOW, THE DAY is mine, ours, not somebody else's. You never feel alone with a donkey. He never imposes his will on you. I sense his rustling presence, his loyalty, even as I drift off, as I wander, as I doodle in my mind. I'm jolted out of a daydream if he halts for a tasty morsel, for something green. I let him eat what he wants today; in return, he takes me where I want to go. We walk together through a tunnel of sand-colored earth, throbbing in incandescent yellow. Soon the forest opens out into a large meadow, a kind of dell, bereft of trees, full of cows and sheep glowing in emerald luminosity. We're on our way to Le Brignon.

There's a brook trundling across our path, with a stone bridge to cross over, a bridge we need to traverse. Suddenly Gribouille stops dead, freezes on its threshold. It's little more than a yard in width, with a six-foot span; he doesn't buy it. I let the lead rope go; he retreats, steps backward, by his own volition. He surveys the problem. His ears are really pricked up and he stands tall. He's a big donkey when he's upright and ready for action. He isn't nervous, merely cautious. He walks around to where the brook is running, to a little stream amid some rocks, easy to step across. Barely would anybody get wet. But Gribouille doesn't like water, not at all. He doesn't much like this option either. He's stopped again, waiting, wondering what to do next...

The situation reminds me of Buridan's Ass, the paradox named after Jean Buridan, the fourteenth-century French cleric and philosopher, a forebear of the scientific revolution, an anticipator of Newtonian theory. Perhaps my mind's going too far, playing tricks on me under the sun. Perhaps I'm just hungry and thirsty. But Buridan's paradox says that a thirsty and hungry donkey placed exactly between two piles of hay of equal size and quality, with a pail of water next to each, would necessarily starve to death through inaction, through not knowing which pile and pail to gobble and drink first. The donkey can't decide between these two options because each possibility is of equal merit, equally enticing—or, in the case of a footbridge and brook, equally hazardous. He'd stand there and eventually die.

Buridan didn't conceive this paradox. It was Aristotle who thought it up in *De Caelo*, posing the same dilemma with respect to a man. It was Buridan's solution to Aristotle that got later satirized, satirized with the addition of an "ass," to emphasize its absurdity. For Buridan, human will would offset any hasty decision, allowing a thinking person, equipped with moral determinism, to reflect upon which course of action serves the greater good, makes the most sense. He'd make no decision until he's fully assessed all the possible outcomes, and all the drawbacks, of making one choice over another. In other words, an entirely rational man, while pondering on what he should do next, would, in the long run, perish. Two hundred years later, Spinoza chipped into the debate by saying: "I readily grant that a man placed in such a state of equilibrium ... would die of hunger and thirst. If they ask me whether such a man is not to be reckoned an ass rather than a man, I reply that I do not know, just as I do not know how one should reckon a man who hangs himself, or how one should reckon babies, fools, and madmen."

I don't know either. But I have an idea here, a rational one, I suppose. I'll simply walk across the bridge myself, and then return. I'll walk back and forth, back and forth, making sure Gribouille is watching. So back and forth I go, and watch me he does. See, it's safe to cross. His reactions are amazing. He absolutely knows what I'm doing. He looks very alert. Those ears are almost vertical now, and he's standing attentively, almost studiously. In Buridan's ass paradox, the commentators state the ass simply *sits* pondering what to do next. Of course, a donkey would never sit down in such a situation, nor would he spend too much time assessing the options. He'd merely wander elsewhere to eat some other greenery, and soon forget about the piles of hay. The other thing to note is that donkeys often *smell* their food before they see it, and hence where they stick their muzzle is often conditioned by smell rather than sight. Indeed, their sensory system is more highly developed than any philosopher's, with their big brain attuned only to abstract reasoning.

After about three crossings, I retake the lead rope, put my hand on Gribouille's poll, stand tightly next to him, feeling his warmth, and walk. *Allez-hop!* We walk over the footbridge, slowly. In all, it takes us less than ten seconds. Traverse it we do; the problem was a molehill rather than a mountain. Together we've resolved Buridan's paradox! Which begs the question: what would Gribouille have done if I'd *not* led him across? How would he, alone, have confronted things? My immediate response is that he'd probably never have gotten himself in that position in the first place, probably not wandered halfway across France with a pile of bags on his back, trying to cross a little bridge. He wouldn't have traveled that far, placed himself in that perceived danger. It was *me* who led him there, *me* who wanted him to cross the obstacle. The bridge posed no danger to a human, so what was his problem? Perhaps I was the problem?

Thus, Buridan's ass has nothing to do with donkeys. It's *we* who've framed the paradox, conceived a problem, and proposed a solution, a solution *acceptable* to us, not to a donkey, a solution made at their expense. I remember what Ben Hart told me when I went to Sidmouth: donkeys aren't good at solving the problems we've posed, at resolving things in human terms. As for logic, or even mathematics—Euclid's fifth geometrical proposition, after all, is called *Pons Asinorum*—the "Bridge of Asses" (often the "Bridge of Fools")—I think again of John Fowles, writing in *The French Lieutenant's Woman:* "Sarah *was* intelligent, but her real intelligence belonged to a rare kind; one that would certainly pass undetected in any of our modern tests of faculty. It was not in the least analytical or problem-solving, and it is no doubt symptomatic that the one subject that had cost her agonies to master was mathematics. It was rather an uncanny ability to classify other people's worth: to understand them, in the fullest sense of that word." Her obstinacy was her only succor, a donkey's only succor for survival, for always having a third option up their muzzle.

14

WE WALK THROUGH sheep and cows, through a hazy late-afternoon quiver that drifts over the meadow. Gribouille drinks in the pure essence of summer, snorts and tiptoes over the soft earth. I follow. I inhale and exhale, taking in a big gulp of rurality, of a bleating, mooing air full of manure. We exchange glances and offer each other company, a quiet communion in August. He pauses momentarily to stand to attention: head down, hooves together to the front and back, responsive to some otherworldly command I can't quite hear, can't quite fathom. My hand returns to his poll, and we're moving again. We pass one herd of cows and they become agitated and frisky, breaking the silence.

This has happened before. Gribouille has that effect on cows: they run over, fast, faster than you'd ever believe cows could run, and leap about wildly, almost frenziedly, edging up to the barbed-wire fence, staring intently, madly, at Gribouille. What's bothering them, exactly? It's hard to tell. A slumbering brown donkey and a *trapu* man in a blue-flannel shirt? Gribouille veers over to the other side of the track, away from the cows, and stops again to eat. He looks neither up nor over at the cows. He knows they're there because he's purposely changed tack; yet he seems typically unperturbed. His calmness is a miracle to behold, and sort of infectious. Even when dogs come raging toward us, baring their fangs, beside him I fear nothing. I remain tranquil and we amble unhurried through the barking din.

Some dogs are friendlier and curious. They wander up tentatively, nervously, and start barking. But it's so often a bark that wants to say hello, that wants to tell you that life's a bit quiet around here and he's glad of some company, happy a few new faces are passing through the village. One dog has been following us for a while, a little black-and-white terrier, an affectionate farmer's mutt. I'm content to have a third wanderer but wonder when he's going to turn back, return home. I bend down and give him the odd stroke; he rolls over on his back in the sunshine, begging me to tickle his warm belly. He's there now, twenty meters ahead of us, leading the way. He's really fascinated by Gribouille and bounds up, though never gets too close because of trepidation. Gribouille taunts him playfully with his muzzle. When Gribouille stops to take his *feed*, the dog lies tummy-down along the path. If the path is gravelly and runs down an incline, he lets himself slide front-first like a canine toboggan slithering through fresh snow, giving himself a glorious scratch in the process. After about an hour in our company, the mutt suddenly turns around and scoots off.

Sheep gravitate toward Gribouille as well. They usually scatter when humans approach. With a donkey, they come over, actively want to seek us out. We're a traveling minstrel show, a couple of medieval troubadours hopping from one village to another, wandering through dells and dingles, entertaining humans and animals alike, playing a curious folk music people want to hear. It's an amazing turnabout. We were walking through a little rundown hamlet the other day, passing by a farm shed that I thought contained cows. It turned out to be crammed with sheep, with ewes and little lambs that poked their baldy heads out the door, peering underneath their pen. Beady eyes dying to catch a glimpse of Gribouille. Unlike with cows, Gribouille stopped, stood up tall, raised his ears, and somehow took note. He wandered right up to the shed door. He was transfixed for an instant, statuesque in his inspection and in his introspection. Nothing happened apart from some cosmic animal kinesis.

৵৵

Bridge of Fools, Buridan's Ass . . . all used pejoratively, all used to denote something dumb . . . The chestnuts abound. The denigration of the donkey was apace early. Circa 600 B.C., the Greek sage Aesop wrote hundreds of fabled *Fables*, little nuggets of wisdom and secret meaning; and yet almost all of these sly parables, if they use donkeys—asses—allegorically, do so scathingly, ignorantly and unjustly. It's a mystery why a man born a slave, who raised himself from a position of servility to one of renown, should betray the humble beast-of-burden underdog, someone he'd once resembled.

Take the fable of "The Ass's Brains," in which the lion and fox go hunting together. The lion, following the fox's advice, sends a message to an ass, hoping he'll broker their alliance. Overjoyed, the ass rushes to the spot of rendezvous, where the lion immediately pounces. Here's our dinner tonight, he tells the fox. Then the lion leaves the fox to watch over the ass. But he's away awhile, and soon, in the lion's absence, the fox picks out the ass's brains and eats them up. The lion comes back, sees the lack of ass's brains, and demands: "What have you done with the brains?" "Brains, your Majesty!" says the fox, "it had none, or it would never have fallen into your trap." Moral: "Wit has always an answer ready."

Then there's "The Ass in the Lion's Skin," where an ass puts on a lion's skin and roams the forest frightening

other animals. He encounters a fox, whom the ass likewise tries to scare. But the fox heard the sound of an ass's
voice, and exclaimed: "I might possibly have been frightened myself, if I had not heard your bray." Moral: "Clothes
may disguise a fool, but his words will give him away."
And in "The Ass and the Grasshopper," the chirping of
grasshoppers enchants an ass. He desires the same melodic charms, and wonders what sort of food they eat to
maintain such beautiful voices, such lush tonalities. "The
dew," the grasshoppers say. Resolved to mimic the grasshoppers, the ass decides to live only upon the dew, yet in a
short while dies of hunger. Moral: "Even a fool is wise—
when it is too late."

I remember feeling foolish and humiliated once,
Gribouille, when I was young, very young, when I was
least equipped to respond; I could've been a pilloried ass
in any Aesop fable. I would've been about ten years old. I
had these thick-lens glasses because my eyesight was bad.
I sat in front of four or five men who asked me questions,
tested me, tried to catch me out, laughing, barely guard-
edly, under their breaths, behind a big wooden desk in an
old, stuffy, headmaster's office. I sat there stammering,
muttering the wrong responses inarticulately, nervously,
glowing red, trying to gain entry to their grammar school,
trying to go above my station, wearing lion's clothing. I
failed, needless to say. But the worst thing was that it
wasn't really me being tested; it was my parents, who were
both present, sitting at the back of the room, watching
me suffer, unable to speak a word, perhaps feeling humiliated themselves, because they'd have fared no better

than me. It was a lesson in class, *social class*, scripted the English way.

You see, neither my parents or I knew the ropes, read books, had the right inflections, possessed the correct etiquette. It was our "natural" disadvantage, like being born a donkey, like entering the world to seek misfortune. In families of the rich, there's not the same self-doubt and weakness, the same propensity for humiliation, whose fathers and mothers went to college, had books in their big houses, who became officers—not cannon-fodder—in wars. My father's brother never returned from service in Italy, blown up in a tank, in November 1943, his first trip abroad, a sunny vacation cut short, aged eighteen, a volunteer. My mother and father were both forced to quit school at the age of twelve because of that war, because of the air raids, when they were evacuated to the countryside. When it was over, returning to a bomb-damaged Liverpool, it was time to start work, and too late for an education, too futile.

After my mother's death, a nasty death from lung cancer, a decade back, I found among her possessions the beginnings of a story she was writing on her family, really about her grandmother, "the greatest influence on my childhood," trailing off at an unlucky page thirteen. Born the seventh child of an Irishman from Athlone and a Welsh mother from Beaumaris, one day my mother's grandmother's father, a rope-maker, decided to immigrate to America, taking with him his four eldest daughters. He couldn't afford the whole family. Quickly, he decided the New World wasn't to his liking, and returned home, leaving his four girls behind. He didn't last long back home, though, since pneumonia saw him off at age forty. Thereafter, it was my mother's grandmother, her "Nin," house-cleaner for rich merchants, who raised the family, including the one my mother would be born into, living in her grandmother's tiny inner-city row house . . .

I'm not sure why I'm telling you all this, Gribouille, why I think it's relevant. I give a gentle jolt on the lead rope, and Gribouille responds, giving a sly glance in my direction. There are things I need to tell him, things perhaps he already knows, already suspects . . . Maybe it's because I'm secretly proud of my humble roots, because I feel more affinity with you, Gribouille, than with somebody for whom life has been served up on a silver platter, or deposited in a trust fund. Perhaps I'm glad I was humiliated at the age of ten. It wised me up, let me know on which side of the fence I stood, would always stand: with the donkeys or with the masters?

Perhaps it's why I privately revel in how things have changed, in how I did eventually go to college, how I studied hard, read everything, toiled long in my simple wooden chair, dug a groove in its cushion I sat so long. I've still got it; I can show you the groove. I imbibed everything in my room, sat at my desk, in this chair. Now I'm better qualified than that interview panel, than those who denied me entry to their school. Now I've glimpsed their world, from within. Now I'm clever enough to know that I no longer want entry: they can keep it for themselves. Now I'm smarter and stronger than them, more determined, more driven. Harboring a grudge? I can't escape it. The scars are there, Gribouille, they'll always be there.

15

A DONKEY HAS a pain threshold that's staggering; they'll often struggle on, no matter how mistreated, no matter how fatigued they are. In a strange way, they might carry on only to be stubborn, only to show that nothing is hurting, though a lot is really hurting. "A donkey hides pain," the Sidmouth Sanctuary donkey vet Alex Thiemann told me during my sojourn there. "They internalize pain," she said, "bow their heads, grin and bear, and often do nothing that outwardly shows their stress. Horses buck up, rear, kick and make a grand fuss if they're in pain. With a donkey, it's the complete opposite, and so it's difficult for a vet to spot immediately that there's something up." Hence it *appears* that donkeys feel no pain.

The pages of the scholarly *Equine Veterinary Journal* confirm as much: the lack of visible expression of pain in a donkey hampers veterinary diagnosis. Signs aren't suspected until terminal stages of disease. Horses in severe or acute pain demonstrate recognizable changes in behavior, whereas donkey behavioral changes are subtler, more restrained. Vets point to their stoic and sedate

nature, to their reluctance to express signs of pains be-
haviorally, and to the part played by evolution: the species
has survived by masking or minimizing signs of pain, so
reducing a predator's advantage, so feigning possible vulnerability. Commonly reported hints of problems are
lethargy and reduced alertness, self-isolation or facing
away from handlers, and lower-head carriage. Violent and
frequent rolling in the earth might mean severe abdominal pain, pain rather than happiness, perhaps colic; cautious or very slow chewing on a favored side hints of
mouth or teeth problems; altered weight distribution in
standing postures and slight gait changes suggest foot or
leg-joint pains.

A donkey's emotional pain is equally subtle, especially when they've lost a companion or longstanding
friend. Donkeys' psychic needs are very complex. They
don't like being fielded alone and it's very rare, and often
very wrong, to see it. Donkeys forge strong bonds with
other donkeys, indeed with other animals, and if that
partner dies, the surviving donkey must be allowed to
mourn, must be allowed to come to terms with any loss,
somehow. A donkey can spend days and days searching
for a missing loved one; and if too perplexed by what's
happened, by an inexplicable absence, they can go into a
deep depression and eventually die themselves, tragically,
of a broken heart. It's a history of love and devotion that
could fill the annals of romantic poetry; and it's dramatized some classic pieces of prose.

Cervantes highlights a few tender moments between
Dapple and Rocinante, Don Quixote's steed, and the

wisdom we humans can extract from such dedicated camaraderie, from so firm a friendship. These two friends,
Cervantes says, "used to approach and rub each other, most
lovingly, and after they'd rested and refreshed themselves,
Rocinante would lay his neck across Dapple's—it would
extend almost half a meter on the other side—and staring
intently at the ground, the two of them could stand this
way for three days or, at least, for as long as they were per-
mitted to do so or were not compelled by hunger to look
for food." "I say, then, that ... we can infer, to widespread
admiration, how deep the friendship of these two peaceable animals must have been, to the shame of human
beings who do not know how to maintain their friend-
ships."

Our lack of trust, our inability to maintain friend-
ships, is something George Orwell tried to figure out centuries later in *Animal Farm,* his brilliant satire on *human*
hypocrisy and political machination. The book's most
intriguing character, Benjamin, is, remember, a donkey,
with a complex emotional life. He's the oldest and savviest
animal on the farm and best friend of the carthorse,
Boxer. Benjamin seldom talked and never laughed: he
found little in life to laugh about. If he did say something,
it was usually a gloomy, cryptic remark—"for instance, he
would say that God had given him a tail to keep the flies
off, but that he would sooner have no tail and no flies." Or:
"Donkeys live a long time. None of you has ever seen a
dead donkey." Benjamin could read very well, but never
exercised his faculty. "So far as he knew, he said, there was
nothing worth reading." And yet, although he never openly

admitted it, Benjamin was utterly devoted to Boxer. The two of them "usually spent their Sundays together in the small paddock beyond the orchard, grazing side by side and never speaking."

This pair of veterans dreamed of retiring together one day, of peacefully scratching each other's back somewhere safe, in the corner of a big green pasture; until, that is, Boxer collapses through overwork, building the farm's windmill. Benjamin had always urged Boxer to work less hard, warned him to take care of his health. "A horse's lungs do not last forever." Before he's eventually whisked off to the knackers' yard, before he's ground into bone meal, Benjamin lies down at Boxer's side, "and, without speaking, kept the flies off him with his long tail." All the animals were astonished to see Benjamin galloping one day, like never before, braying at the top of his voice. It was the first time they'd ever seen him so excited, the first time they'd seen him gallop. "Quick, quick!" Benjamin shouted. "Come at once! They're taking Boxer away!"

"Fools! Fools," bawled Benjamin at the other animals waving good-bye, stamping the earth with his small hooves. "Fools! Do you not see what is written on the side of the van? 'Alfred Simmonds, Horse Slaughterer and Glue Boiler, Willingdon, Dealer in Hides and Bonemeal.'" After Boxer's death, the mourning Benjamin became even more morose and taciturn than ever. He was on to the hypocrisy of events well before anybody else, and the only animal unmoved by the revolution. No matter what, Benjamin said, life would go on as it had always gone on—which is to say, badly.

It was Benjamin, too, who finally consented to break his rule, reading out those fateful lines written on the wall: "ALL ANIMALS ARE EQUAL, BUT SOME ARE MORE EQUAL THAN OTHERS." None of the other animals knew what this meant, except Benjamin, "who nodded his muzzle with a knowing air ..." Benjamin and Boxer's last moments together are a tender personal finale to a parable of brutal, abstract world history, of carting people off to the knackers' yard. Perhaps that's Orwell's point: the real meaning of life is found in companionship, in love and devotion, not in politics—nor in geometry and mathematics. All that sort of gets in the way.

16

THE HAUTE-LOIRE IS full of loyal partnerships, of bedbugs passed between peaceable pals. It has been a favorite pastime of mine in free afternoons, and no funding is necessary: *donkey spotting*, scouring the landscape in search of wagging tails and flapping ears, of particular little stationary dots in the distance. I've done a lot of this investigative research on my bike, because I can cover many miles at a time, yet cruise slow enough to watch out, to keep my eyes peeled for possible sightings, for new acquaintances and charming camaraderie. I can lose myself along lonely lanes where only tractors chug by once in a while, climb mountain passes that lead only upward, journey off-road

down dusty tracks that end only in unending forest laby-
rinths. Almost always there'll be donkeys, and their friends,
awaiting me around a turn.

I can spot a donkey a mile off. There's something
about its movements, about its motionless presence, its
bowed head in the earth. I've seen male Jacks and female
Jennys, castrated Geldings and all-male Stallions, packs
of males and females and foals grooming one another,
rolling around together in the dirt; I've seen horses with
donkeys, a donkey happily fielded with a group of cows,
about five in all, in a field along the Route Nationale 102,
on the way to Brioude, in full view of tourists speeding to
and from the south, a light-brown donkey, content as can
be. He sits among his black-and-white friends on the hillside, flicking around his ears, swishing away the flies,
happy knowing company is nearby; and if I bike up a
steep hill beyond the village of Saint Cirgues, past a field of
vines, there's a wonderful old chocolate-colored male
whose best friend is an equally ancient ram, a ram with a
limp, curly horns, and a shaggy matted coat.

He's a wise old dreadlocked ram who spends his days
meditating underneath his best friend the donkey, literally underneath, loyally following him wherever he goes,
hobbling a step behind along the narrow paths that criss-
cross the valley. They're winding down their last years
together, just as Benjamin and Boxer had hoped to do.
Donkeys are known to be faithful protectors, loyal surrogate guard dogs for sheep (and goats), befriending them,
bedding down with them at night, bonding, braying to
fend off canine predators. The ram skids off when I arrive,

fearful of humans. But the donkey sticks his big brown head over the fence and lets me shoo away the flies, caress his graying brow. He's an affectionate lad, as docile and as lovable as they come. Meanwhile, the ram stands guard a few yards to the rear, eying me quizzically, suspiciously, surveying my interactions with his friend. As I depart, remounting my bike, the ram returns to the haven of his four-legged shelter. This duet of calm is an endearing vision. I head off in the sunshine, over the hills, feeling better about the world, heartened by the curious gratitude I feel for a ram and a donkey in a quiet field.

This ram and donkey get me to thinking about Dapple and Sancho, and about my own relationship with you, Gribouille. The bond between humans and donkeys is necessarily understated. A donkey's modus operandi is based upon *discretion,* done on the sly, in private. There's an unwritten agreement between both parties wherein equal rights and duties prevail, things to learn and stuff to teach, for man and beast alike. Sancho found stability and strength with Dapple, shelter from the hailstone of rocks that life incurs. Sometimes, the shelter Dapple gave Sancho was real. When Ginés de Pasamonte hurls rocks at Don and Sancho, the former "could not shield himself as well as Sancho," because Sancho "hid behind his donkey," who, "pensive, with bowed head, twitched his ears from time to time," characteristically taking a battering without complaint. If, as *Don Quixote* implies, human life is really one of *defeat,* of tragic failure, then the best we can find is a little shelter under our donkey, a safe haven from the rocks, a little bit of everyday loyalty in a world that's gone haywire.

Dapple is Sancho's equal, a mirror of Sancho's own uncomplicated self. Sancho's tenderest moments are with his donkey; and he's happiest riding, full-belly, sidesaddle on his Dapple, "not caring at all about finding greater fortune." Frequently, talking to Dapple makes more sense than talking to his master, the Don, because Dapple helps Sancho bear his misfortunes, speaks the simple language of patience and peace. It's a hard thing to do, says Sancho, speaking your mind to someone: "a man searches his whole life and doesn't find anything but kicks and tossings in a blanket, stones and fists hitting him, and still he has to keep his mouth shut tight, not daring to say what's in his heart, like a mute." With a donkey, he utters an honest, naïve truth.

17

DOWN THE LANE I hear a car approaching us, driving off-road, rough track, getting nearer and nearer: we're headed in its direction. Then it comes into sight and stops a little way in front of us. A man gets out, an elderly man, who walks toward us. Gribouille stops to eat, carelessly. "Have you seen a black horse?" the man shouts at me. "She's broken from her field down there, and has been running wild for a while now. She's lost somewhere." I've seen nothing; I tell him I've seen nothing, and nobody. *Rien.* Sorry.

I quickly forget about the man and the horse. I'm

walking toward Sembadel, winding along a trail between shrubs and fields. I start walking down into a little hamlet, a couple of houses, when suddenly I see a black horse in a field. I get closer and closer and realize the horse is in a field without any fences, that it's roaming free, that it's the horse who's lost, who's running wild. Then it comes bounding toward us, friskily, nervously. It makes me nervous. I start to get anxious. Gribouille senses something, too, senses me reacting. He stirs a little, pricks up his ears, lifts his head, and halts.

The horse is young and very agitated. She's galloping now; and then, near us, starts to rear. I'm definitely not happy, a little fearful, scared: I don't know how to handle a loose horse. She quietens for a moment, and horse and donkey sniff one another. I try to edge Gribouille away, around the horse, passing over the field; but the horse blocks our path and rears again, towering over both of us. Gribouille has none of this, and walks away in the opposite direction, into another field, and starts to bury his head in the earth, eating, seemingly forgetting what's happening. I don't know how, but somehow I've lost the lead rope. When a donkey faces an unfamiliar situation, they'll usually try to walk away from it; if it's really threatening, they'll run away. I try not to panic too much.

I'm confronted with the problem: what to do? Each time I try to approach Gribouille, to reclaim the lead rope, the horse seems to go for *me*. She kicks out in my direction, at me—not good. It's me she doesn't like, me who's getting in the way of her little fling with my donkey. We play this game for a while. Each time I approach Gribouille, the horse rears up; and each time, my donkey walks away. I can't get near him now. Before long, I realize he's *protecting* me; he seems to know that the horse has a problem with me. In turning his back on me, in walking away, it seemed that Gribouille is being loyal, a good companion, sort of taking care of me. It's hard to know for sure. But we're all locked into a stalemate. Nobody is going anywhere. I stop to watch the horse and donkey together and begin to regain my calm, slowing things down, taking deep breaths underneath my breath. Gribouille plainly isn't interested in the horse, yet the horse persists in poking around. Then, after about fifteen minutes, I finally see a car arriving down the lane, the same car as earlier, with, happily, the same driver, here to recapture his horse. I wave, utter words of relief, shake his hands. He puts a halter on his young mare and walks her away. The incident is over.

Afterward, once back walking, I reflect upon what happened, and how I sort of panicked. The horse knew it and got even edgier. Gribouille, alone, stayed calm, walked away, let the situation wash over him without too much bother. I had a lot to learn about dealing with tricky situations, even minor ones. Little wonder that for their calming effects donkeys are sometimes fielded with nervous horses or can become supervisors in halter breaking, when a donkey wears a collar that's attached to the halter of a young calf or yearling horse; the young rookie has no option but to follow the donkey around, and it's the donkey who thus performs the tricky lead training. Likewise, if a donkey is introduced to a mare and a foal during weaning, the foal will often turn to the donkey for support after it has left its mother. The donkey's calmness is passed on to the foal, and the trauma of the separation is lessened. Patience and calm go a long way in everybody's well-being, in dealing with fear, in reacting without overreacting, in alleviating stress, in making clearheaded decisions. It's easier said than done, I know, and when a horse rears up, right in front of you, and starts kicking out, all I could think about was being kicked into a pulp, like the rogue in Daudet's tale, with a feather spinning around in the breeze, all that's left of me in a very lonely country death.

Several days later, another incident, again with a horse, ditto a stray horse. Owners really need to keep a check on their enclosures, repair them regularly, because this time two horses had broken loose, two big fellows. Keep calm, like Gribouille! We'd come too far over the hillock to go back; it'd be a pain retracing our steps, to opt to avoid the issue at hand. We had no choice but to confront them, unflinchingly, with authority, to walk right through them, plot a course through this Scylla and Charybdis. This was the path we *needed* to take. So, tightening Gribouille's lead rope, with my arm around his neck, this time I walked directly toward the horses. The lane was barely ten feet across. I continued to walk, standing my ground, sticking to the middle of the route, trying to control my heartbeat, staying in control, very close to Gribouille, whom I felt I needed to protect. He kept his muzzle low, compliantly. The horses watched us for an instant, then suddenly reared and ran off.

They didn't come back. We walked together, without glancing back. Gribouille kept moving, cognizant of what was going on; he made no attempt to dart for food. He stayed tranquil as before, as with the stray black horse. Yet this situation became *no* situation because I didn't panic; I went forward slowly, cautiously, with surety, like a donkey. The horses sensed this, and I'm certain Gribouille could tell the difference. He went with me because he felt safe, protecting me just as he knew I was protecting him. He had no need to run, to flee the danger, like before. He was teaching me calm; and I showed him how to problem-solve through calm. Running away is natural behavior for a donkey faced with a threatening problem, just as it's hard for any human to stand still in a scary situation; standing still isn't "normal" behavior for an equine, and evolution hasn't favored those who stuck around and waited while a predator closed in. And yet, teaching a donkey to stand still, showing them there's nothing to fear, staying close by, touching them, moving slowly with them, all this revealed that if they stand still, or don't run away, scary things might stop.

It was a win-win solution, if we put our minds together. I let myself go with him and he, in turn, trusts my confidence, enters into a tactile dialogue with me. We become at one with each other. I concentrate fully on my donkey, on what needs to be done to work together, to solve the problem. I don't rush ahead. I start to mimic the donkey disposition, reach a state of calm void rather than hollow emptiness, a feeling that everything I have, everything I own or wear, all of it, equates to nothing. I'm just concentrating with him, alongside him. There's no past or future, just here and now, an absolute present. I'm simply *there*, naked like him: a donkey who wears no clothes, who has no money, who eats and drinks, who seems to take everything in his stride. I'm what I am right there, nothing more, just a singular self. If you let yourself drift into that donkey world, taking simple little strides and slow deep breaths, calm reigns. Things happen with clarity, with simplicity, decisively—like eating dandelions.

18

THE DEW DROP, the crystal of life, the dawn distilled. It's the hour to saddle up. I'm standing next to a road in a damp farmer's field. Gribouille is sniffing a sheep dog called Février, who's mesmerized by my partner. A car passes once in a while toward Bellevue-la-Montagne. The sky is overcast. It's a lot cooler, and the early morning air enters my veins like a cold cascade tumbling through a craggy crevice. I spent last night in the company of Michel and Françoise, at their modest *chambre d'hôte*, ate well with them, a gratin with lots of potatoes, and drank *vin ordinaire* out of a little tumbler, sleeping soundly in a guest room with a double bed and not much else. They were inquiring about my trek, wanted to hear all about it, and about this book I'm meant to be writing. Michel, who's not much older than me, raises dairy cows, has thirty or so *bêtes,* for milk he sells to a local cooperative at a guaranteed price; the milk goes toward Saint Agur—a strong, creamy blue cheese fabricated in the nearby Velay mountains.

They're both surprised that I know the area so well. I told them I've walked the trails around here many times before, usually without a donkey. I first came here about five years ago now, I said. There was a philosopher, somebody named Guy Debord, who once lived down the road, reclusively, in Champot, a neighboring hamlet, about a mile away, in a house surrounded by a high stone wall. He killed himself there, a decade or more back, a bullet in the heart, like van Gogh. Michel knew of this man, even saw him a few times, always dressed in black, and had his own stories to share with me—rumors, village gossip, hearsay. This philosopher had interested me a lot, I said, perhaps too much. I'd read his work and wanted to see this lonely house that he'd claimed "opened directly onto the Milky Way."

He'd called the region "a land of storms," because of the storms that move in rapidly, usually in late afternoon, especially in summer, catching you unaware. It hails golf balls sometimes. They caught me unaware once, defenseless, without shelter, as lightning struck a nearby telegraph pole, not twenty yards away; an absolutely deafening crack, a sudden flash, for a startling instant. A couple of seconds of pure terror: "They would approach noiselessly at first, announced by a brief passage of wind that slithered through the grass or by sudden flashes on the horizon; then thunder and lightning were unleashed, and we were bombarded for a long while and from every direction, as if in a fortress under siege."

🌿

I guess I was still in my "other-person's-life" phase back then, still searching for something through others, since I'd ideas of writing my own book on this philosopher, a book that never worked out well. So one spring day, on the wooden floor of my New York apartment, I spread out a Michelin map of France's Auvergne region, a very detailed map, taking up almost the entire floor space. I pored over it for hours, trawled through endless place names, pinpointing mile upon mile of the Haute-Loire, doing it until I was giddy and goggle-eyed. I knew it was a rural hamlet, knew this place was called Champot, knew it was where this man came in the twilight of his life, to escape Paris, to escape the world; yet still it eluded me. Before long, I felt like I already knew the entire *département* intimately: there was CHAMPEIX, CHAMPSIAUX, CHAMBON and CHAMPIONG, but no CHAMPOT!

Then I searched the Internet and downloaded numerous commentaries on this man, with allusions to Champot: "It was isolated ... it was deserted ... he had a farmhouse there ..." But where the hell was it? One article said near Champot you got a "fine view of the mountains." So I returned to the map and narrowed down the hunt, focusing on mountainous spots, on pinholes where the contours narrowed and the altitude increased. Alas, nothing. Then it occurred to us that maybe, just maybe, somebody was translating a little too much. Maybe, in fact, "fine view of the mountains" was really a place name, not a perspective. *Voilà!* I began to make progress: sure enough, Bellevue-la-Montagne was there on the map. It was a place, a real village, and high up. Champot was supposedly in its shadow, but *where* precisely?

Undeterred and undaunted, I set off across the Atlantic, pursuing this man's spirit, perhaps fleeing my own, maybe searching for it, jetting off chasing weird ghosts, exorcising phantoms of my imagination. I arrived at Lyon's Saint-Exupéry Airport, hired a car, and, like a *petit prince*, journeyed to a remote microworld far from planet Earth. The Michelin map led me, though somehow the notion of direction lost all sense of meaning. I knew only up and down, forward and backward, journeying for miles and miles along narrow country roads, winding and wending my way across Auvergne countryside, down in valleys, up over mountains, through remote villages, traversing time and space, onward toward some distant inland shore. At one point, after hours of driving, I feared the worst: I was lost. But then, further up one meandering tree-lined lane, I had a break: at the roadside I spotted an old, worn way-stone inscribed with the following: "BELLEVUE 8 km."

I entered Bellevue itself, via the main road, stopping at the butcher's shop, the only open store, really the only *petit commerce* left in a village the world no longer needs. Amazingly, *madame la patronne*, Madame Soulier, I later learned, not only knew Champot, she even drew me a little map. She'd eventually become a confidante in my mad caper. And soon I stood in Champot, a little cluster of three or four farmhouses. It felt very far from anywhere, two universes away from Manhattan's Upper West Side, where I'd set out fifteen hours earlier. I hadn't felt such magical warm silence for years; perhaps it was the first time I'd ever felt it.

The following summer, I came back to Champot, installing myself in a house down the lane at Champot Bas, the lower hamlet. I'd seen it advertised on the Web, a summer home for rent near Bellevue. I couldn't believe it. It turned out to be a couple of hundred yards from Champot, and apparently available. I tried to call the owner, but the line was dead. I tried again at different times, checked the code, everything. No avail. Maybe the ad was out of date? Then I decided to write to *le maire* at Bellevue's town hall. For months I heard nothing. Then, one day, out of the blue, a letter arrived from Champot Bas, a handwritten note from the proprietor of the *gîte*, giving details and rates and thanking me for my interest. I wasted no time confirming the reservation, and to Champot I went, again—and again, as it happened, the year after. There, during long, quiet summer days, I became a transformed man, never the same.

I began to understand the real conditions of my life, prompting me to take the plunge, to quit my career as a scholar for hire. Too much stagnant water had doused flames that once burned brightly. I became a shipwrecked pirate who'd actually found his island paradise, his bounty after the mutiny. During that second summer, during the *canicule,* I met this philosopher's widow, sat with her in a shaded spot in the garden, inside the high wall, around a

circular table with a green tablecloth. She smoked a ciga-
rillo, offered me wine, spoke frankly about her late husband. There'd been something about the Gallic simplicity
and style, the richness of its basic value system, without
ostentation, that helped convince me, helped convert me. I
guess I wanted my own shaded round table covered with a
green cloth; I guess I wanted my own life to look out onto
the Milky Way.

19

AFTER BIDDING MICHEL and Françoise *au revoir*, promising to return soon, I hugged Gribouille. I'd spent some
happy moments at Champot, but I couldn't relive them. I
had to let them pass, had to let this philosopher go, had to
scour the universe for new twinkling stars. I'm reassured
knowing Gribouille is by my side for another day on foot,
going forward somewhere else. But I still vividly remember what I did after that meeting with this philosopher's
widow. I went for a walk, not long before sunset, in a rich
golden light. I'd stopped on a rock to unwind, sitting down
to contemplate, to clear my head, listening to the chorus
of birds.

The rock wasn't far from Le Monthiol, where I'm
headed now, a tiny community, a kind of rural idyll,
nestled between meadows and woods, far from any main
road. Marcel, a diminutive septuagenarian, resides there.

After a decade's toil, he has single-handedly built a palatial garden, replete with classical Greek statues and manicured lawns and giant stone mushrooms. He has immortalized the dove, *la colombe,* the bird of peace, as his mascot. Everybody in the commune knows Marcel; Le Monthiol is fêted because of his handy work. Early that evening, I had meditated close by chez Marcel. It was an early-evening contentedness I'd not easily forget.

Gribouille and I stop outside Marcel's house. I'm surprised to see the grass overgrown. Things look a bit disheveled. The hamlet was always small, but it used to feel alive, fresh, and bright. A couple of properties now have their shutters closed and seem empty, bereft of people. Today, under gray skies, the silence is eerie rather than fecund, a little depressing. I attach Gribouille to the gatepost and tell him I won't be long, just a quick call to say *bonjour.* When I visited Le Monthiol those past summers, Marcel would always welcome me into his minute two-up, two-down residence, call me *mon petit,* and fill my glass with huge hits of *pastis;* I'd stagger back to my rented *gîte,* my head dancing a devilish dance, whirling around in the hot air.

I can't disguise my shock. An even more diminutive man greets us, surprised yet pleased, a man whose life force has withered, a pale man who looks like he's soon about to die. He pats Gribouille's front and invites me in. Things haven't been going well, he says; he's tired, he can't keep up the work in the garden, his masterwork; he's going to sell soon. The neighbors are dying around him and their houses are shuttered up. The game's over here, there's no time left, there's too much time. What will happen? He's got cancer. It's clear. I need a few *pastis* this morning, despite the hour, to lift my spirits, to not let my sorrow become too evident. He asks me what I've been doing, what I'm doing with a donkey. I try to explain, pretend to be jolly, normal, but I hear myself laughing awkwardly, being insincere, babbling banalities. I was relieved to exit. Yet once outside, I see Gribouille has done his business outside the front gate. I'd left him there alone too long, irresponsibly, on too short a rope. Don't blame him, because it's my fault. Marcel tells me not to worry, he'll clean up the mess, greater things go wrong ...

I'll never see him again. We both know it. I'll cherish the memories of him looking suntanned, sleeves rolled up, robust, smiling while he got stuck into his wonderful garden, now looking so forlorn. I'll remember the moments I passed there, when he gave me these great piles of lettuces; he had them coming out of his ears, he said, more than he could eat. Needless to say, they tasted incredible, like nothing many people will ever taste in their lifetime. I also remember sending him a postcard, saying hi and thanks from New York, a clichéd picture of the skyline, with the Twin Towers, and receiving a letter in response.

It wasn't really a letter: more a handmade postcard, a picture of his good self with three other locals happily playing *boules* in the yard. In the corner of the photo was another tiny photo he'd clipped on, showing his garden in full bloom, looking resplendent. And attached at the bottom of the main image was yet another tiny image, a simple picture of a plant-pot full of roses, bright red roses. "As you can see," he wrote in his careful cursive, "our village stays mischievous [*coquin*]." "*It's my choice*," he added, in quotation marks, "with this little composition." His little composition, of course, was his garden. Perhaps the hamlet will die off as well now, be another rural casualty, a casualty of time, of old folk dying, of the world changing, of people forgetting, perhaps not wanting to remember...

Gribouille and I walk up an old medieval bridleway, full of loose boulders, and hobble along into Bellevue, past a few defunct cafés—one's called "LA ÉTOILE BLANCHE" ("The White Star"), its sign still visible in upper case. Another is *L'Auberge de la Tour,* a more recent casualty, where I lunched that first bleary-eyed Champot trip. It's midday before I start to feel cheerier, before the sun begins to shine again. But that wonderful summer balminess has gone, given way to a melancholy, to an air of autumn, to *feuilles mortes*...

20

ALL MY ADULT life, I've been bombarded by noise. When I lived in central London, in a little second-floor studio near Russell Square, taxis plagued my nighttime; they seemed to turn the corner underneath my pillow. Where was everybody going? Everywhere was closed. I'd never know, didn't really care. Yet the noise seemed to reverberate directly into *my* living room, tormenting *me* alone. In New York, at Manhattan sidewalk level, a nocturnal rumble activated a chorus call of not-so-neighborly car alarms. They'd get inside your head, under your skin: the band struck up some dumb tune. I willed deafness. When sleep finally came, it was time to collect the garbage. Not much was mine. By day, I was serenaded in stereo: booming rap through one speaker, cellular chatter out of the other, outside my window, discussing stock options. Meanwhile, up above, our neighbor clog-danced from room to room, day and night, night and day. I'd argue with him, threaten him, plead with him . . . One makes a choice to accept this, to normalize it, to desensitize oneself. Or else one leaves.

There were past times when the night alone offered brief solace. That's perhaps why I was a night owl, not the early riser I am now. I was a time-served city boy, even made a sort of career writing and teaching about urban geography, a career I'd ditch, try to shrug off. I found it unfulfilling. Again, I thought it was what I wanted to do with my life. When I went back to college as a second-chance student—a "mature" student, I was called—I always studied at night, burned the midnight oil. For a brief few hours, it was the only time I found quiet. In a dank Oxford college room, amid grime and dust, fading paint and yellowing wallpaper, cobwebs and frayed curtains, I read and wrote in dim light, with darkness outside. Fragments of hush. When daylight came, noise and movement reverberated throughout the flimsy walls and ceilings, everywhere around, above and below, and beside.

The nocturnal habit stuck for a long while. All that time, I never thought I could inhabit anywhere but a big city, never thought I could survive without pacing streets, without staying up late, without cafés and bookstores, without movie houses and bright lights, without constant action, movement, rapidity, people, noise. After a while, daily noise became not only accepted but *necessary*, a hallucinogenic drug you craved, believed you needed, couldn't live without. It was like being online, receiving E-mails: without them, life was empty. Or: there simply was no life. You were dead. Now I'm a night owl in broad daylight, staying mostly off-line. I still call out, in the wind, in the wild, but the tonality is different, less tormented, calmer, a gentle hoot rather than a desperate cry, a lonely sound rather than canned noise.

We're in the silence now, Gribouille and I, within touching distance, feeling distance, breathing distance, in a forest, in a hidden space without gravity, without noise, a secret spiral canal. If I put my finger in my right ear, I can turn the volume down even more. Recently, an ear specialist told me of a hearing loss I have in my left inner ear, a loss he couldn't explain. "What happened?" the doctor quizzed me, upon examining the test results. I didn't know. I may have had it for a long while, since it was only when it got quieter, only when I came to rural France, that I noticed any imbalance. It's specific sounds I can't hear in this ear, specific frequencies, often nice sounds.

I remember *not* hearing one of the nicest sounds of the countryside: the village bells, especially the Sunday morning bells, ringing out as only French village church bells ring out, across the valley, into your bedroom. I was lying in bed during my first week in France. A massive weight had lifted from my life, a blissful relief. Quietness. On my right side, resting my *good* ear on the pillow, I could hear nothing, no chiming bells from Feigères's little *église*, no music playing to the heavens. If I turned on my left side, on the opposite side, I heard, I heard the morning chorus. So I had a good side and a bad side, an ear that heard, an ear that didn't. I thought nothing of it. It was probably the way the wind blew, right? But it happened with the birds, and occasionally with the bees; and, at night, with the crickets, and then with owls, the most comforting bedtime sound. And then with the turtledove . . . I began to suspect something was up. A deafness that downplays only dulcet frequencies. A half-heard ode to joy.

The countryside is full of sounds you hear all the time, sometimes loudly: not only church bells, but birds chirping, insects buzzing, a tractor working in a field, the moo of a cow, a bleat, the call of an owl, a gusting wind, the patter of rain, the hum of *sauterelles* in summer. It's surprising how much sound is around. Yet noise is something other than sound: it's a discordant racket that overlays, and overwhelms, familiar rhythmic tonalities. The difference is instinctive: speeding traffic, car horns, motorbikes, loud music, gunshots, heavy banging, low-flying aircraft—all of which get amplified in environments where restful sound alone prevails.

This lunch spot we've found is next to an old stone bridge, with a narrow hump going over a little stream. I hear the water flowing. It's a lovely little *coin*. I'm hungry. I break up a baguette, a baguette bought that morning from a *new* Bellevue-la-Montagne baker, the first new store to open there for decades—it's not *all* bad news!—and I use my Swiss Army knife to spread duck *rillettes,* locally made, in Chomelix. I'm a king without a kingdom again. I gobble down this luxury without airs or graces. There's a squawking bird, a buzzard—*une buse*—calling a mate overhead, a very distinctive call, a sharp yet somehow acceptable sound.

Then the noise of approaching motocross bikes became palpable. Soon the din is loud and *un*acceptable ... constant revving, ruining fields and tracks, racing over the landscape like it's a play toy, an object of entertainment, for kicking around. That bothers me. It's more than kids having honest fun. Three or four bikes pass over the bridge, jockeying one another; doubtless teenagers on vacation, from the city, from Lyon; soon their machines become fainter and fainter, then progressively louder and louder again as they return, as they head back under the bridge, across the brook. Back and forth they go, loud and quiet. Our stillness is broken. The loud-quiet routine jars on my nerves. I start to feel edgy: I start to feel like I felt when living in a city.

Even Gribouille reacts. He's reacting a bit as Balthazar reacted to the firecrackers at Gérard's raucous party: slightly disgruntled, fidgety at first, only to bury his head in the earth, not letting on, tucking his ears back. Each bang, each rev, prompted a nervous start, a sudden jolt, ever so slightly visible. With their big, floppy ears, donkeys hear very well, better than us. In fact, they have an acute sense of hearing that's used as a kind of visual communication. They'll often hear something, twitch their ears around, tune in, before they actually see anything. (Those ears are also a novel form of air-conditioning, helping donkeys stay cool in warm weather.) It's fascinating, looking at a donkey's ears. Try it sometime. If you caress them yourself, they feel like a baguette fresh out of the oven: warm and soft, yet with a firm texture, a daily bread made from heavenly dough. And watch those baguettes rotate!

They can really swivel, independently, through 180 degrees, via sixteen auricular muscles. Auricular muscles are attached to the base of the external ear, the part we see, the pinna. (We've only three auricular muscles.) Indeed, these baguettes swivel like high-tech antennae, like sensitive microphones: donkeys flick their ears toward the source of any directional sound, to the left or to the right; if the sound comes from the front, they'll prick their ears forward. If sound is too noisy, they can lay their ears back to protect themselves. Where they've got their ears thus illustrates not only what a donkey is listening to; it also signals their emotional state. Pushed-back ears may indicate aggression, a situation with decibels donkeys don't like.

Donkeys hear high-pitched sounds at frequencies closer to 30kHz, an octave higher than us, and can discriminate very small differences in tone and loudness. They can quickly distinguish sound that isn't part of their natural repertoire, and filter it, ignore it, or learn from it.

Donkeys fielded near a main road have been known to bray when they hear the approach of their owner's car, in anticipation of feeding, distinguishing that car from another. Like us, though, a donkey's hearing declines with age, and certain unfamiliar noises can "spook" a donkey. The sound of a motor-cross bike is more than a simple rumble in the countryside: it's a *noise,* something out of place, doubtless heard before by Gribouille; but it's a bad vibe for him, spooky, not an interesting sound. It's a noise that grates against the peace, disturbs both his and my inner harmony, our natural sound system. He's trying not to let it bother him; he's more patient than I am. I can't hold his passive demeanor. We saddle up and leave. I know that I'm perhaps *over*sensitive to noise now. I still have nightmares about London cabs, about New York car alarms, about garbage trucks and insomniacs walking over my head. They're noises that bring about a cold sweat.

21

FADING LIGHT SHINES from a limpid half-moon. The fields look like dark oceans now, stretching off into the night sky, into a transcendent quietude. *Mon ami,* our shelter beckons. Supper dominates my lowly thoughts, and that first hit of cheap country red wine, a glass of *Côtes d'Auvergne,* after walking all day. Some of the nicest *Côtes d'Auvergne* comes from Boudes, a little village in the valley, a regional gem, a well-guarded secret I fear I'm betraying, with its own mild microclimate and stone walls surrounding each vineyard, reminiscent of Burgundy... Now is the hour when Stevenson "drank to the moon's sacred majesty upon the road." It's the hour when I'll soon take my fill. Modestine was inspired "by this purified nocturnal sunshine and bestirred her little hooves as to a livelier measure"; I sense Gribouille is doing something similar, perhaps aware of the impending black curtain descending upon our day. A cool breeze flutters through us, prompting a ghostly dance in the trees, a cracking and a swaying as if someone is up there, lying in hiding, rocking each branch from their lair. I spot two deformed shadows leap out across the gray earth, one with big ears.

And if we look up at the stars, at the heavens, in this living planetarium, we can glimpse two donkeys eating out of a manger, beginning to sparkle as a star cluster: *Asellus Borealis* and *Asellus Australis,* whose Latin names mean "Northern Donkey" and "Southern Donkey." They're almost two hundred light years away, shining at a magnitude of $+4.2$, in the constellation Cancer, the crab: my constellation. Perhaps, then, this voyage, this fantasy, this chance meeting, was always written in the stars, already predestined, always up there in the constellation Cancer, beckoning me, awaiting me? "The starry night," said the philosopher Gaston Bachelard, "is *my* constellation. It makes me aware of *my* power to form constellations. It puts in my hands these weightless chalices and flowers that blossom in space."

Legend has it that the donkeys twinkling in the constellation of Cancer were immortalized by Dionysus, the Greek god of wine, in appreciation for warding off the giants. He and the god of fire, Hephaestus, were riding into battle against the giants, sitting on their donkeys. Soon their mounts began to bray. The giants, never hearing the like before and thinking a terrible monster was about to be unleashed, bade a hasty retreat. Thus Dionysus put the donkeys in the sky, either side of a cluster of stars the Greeks called Phatne, the manger, from which the two donkeys can find permanent feed, ultimate donkey paradise.

Dionysus is so frequently depicted astride a donkey that the donkey is often taken as Dionysus's creature, as having a special affinity with this particular god. Dionysus affirms the life force, implies fecundity and spiritual illumination, divine power and mystical ecstasy. Dionysus was the god who could change water into wine and who granted Midas the infamous power to turn everything he touched into gold. Following the path of Dionysus necessitates forsaking worldly goods, means seeking redemption, perhaps even fleeing on a donkey, on an astral donkey.

Dionysus is called the "twice-born," or the "child of the double door," and symbolizes regeneration and renewal, somebody born again. Conceived out of an affair between Zeus, the mighty god of sky and storms, and the mortal priestess Semele, the fetus Dionysus suffered after his mother asks Zeus to reveal his true character as a god. Zeus desists at first since he knows no mortal can live after bearing witness to a god. Eventually he succumbs and, doing all a god of storms can do, starts pelting Semele with fire and thunderbolts, damning her to the Underworld. Yet to save his son from perishing, Zeus sews the fetus into his testicles, and a few months later Dionysus is miraculously "reborn." This mysterious rebirth, with its differing myths and interpretations, has been worshiped ever since.

The Greek playwright Aristophanes reckoned "the donkey bears the divine mysteries" of the god Dionysus. In Aristophanes' satire *Frogs*, circa 405 B.C., Dionysus and his slave Xanthias are journeying to Hades, on their way to Pluto's court. The play opens with Xanthias atop Dionysus's donkey, shouldering the burden of his master's baggage with a pole. Dionysus is walking alongside when, suddenly, Xanthias begins bemoaning his lot: "Why do I have to pack this stuff around and not have fun like all the other boys?" Dionysus isn't impressed: "Dear me, what airs! What pampered insolence—when Dionysus, Earl of Brandywine, struggles along on foot, and gives his slave a donkey to bear his burden and himself." Xanthias wants his boss to know he's wilting under this weight. And so proceeds the slapstick dialogue:

> Xanthias: "Do *I* not bear it?"
> Dionysus: "How, when you are *borne*?"
> Xanthias: "By carrying *this*."
> Dionysus: "But how ... ?"
> Xanthias: "With pain, *that's* how!"
> Dionysus: "Doesn't the donkey bear the weight *you* bear?"
> Xanthias: "This load I'm toting on my back? No, *sir*!"

Dionysus: "How *can* you tote it when *he's* toting *you*?"
Xanthias: "All I know is, my shoulder's *got the pip!*"
Dionysus: "Well, since the donkey isn't helping you,
suppose you take *your* turn and carry *him*?"

We apparently bear the weight of our existence, but how so, asks Dionysus, when we are *borne* by donkeys, by those dainty legs and little hooves so full of mystery, immortalized in the stars? Suppose we take our turn and carry *him*? Better to be a donkey, quipped another Greek playwright, Menander (circa 340 B.C.), than see a bad man prosper. I can almost glimpse Gribouille nodding his muzzle in agreement. I know I agree and would nod my muzzle if I had one. It's said that humans are more miserable than donkeys because we, at least, are responsible for our cruel fate.

22

A MILKY LIGHT bathes the earth. Night beds down in silent repose. The Northern and Southern donkeys take their evening fill. We're exiting the dirt lane, entering a wider shale track leading up to our lodgings for tonight, another *Chambre d'Hôte.* I feel a chill, a realization that evening is shortening and summer is fading. A melancholy creeps up on me, as a kind of shudder. Perhaps it's tiredness. I start to hear music again. We both hear it, feel it.

It's Schubert, Franz Schubert, that plump, rather shy young man. He suffered periodic moods of depression, drank too much, abused himself, and went inward. A lot of these mood swings and feelings of desolation sprang from this condition, from splitting headaches, from knowing he wouldn't live long.

He wrote some of his best music, music that never earned him a cent, that he never saw published or publicly recognized, when symptoms of syphilis advanced. Yet in the gloom, music rang out, what music from the depths, what sublime creativity, what ecstatic moments, usually as he entertained himself or dazzled a handful of guests and friends at private musical soirées. The posthumously acclaimed Piano Sonata Number 20 (D.959) was written a couple of months before his eventual demise on November 19, 1828. He wrote it while already sick, while living with his brother in a Viennese suburb, where the air was fresher and where the composer could soothe himself walking in nearby countryside.

This four-movement solo piece, with its occasional hammering chords in C-sharp minor, is prodigiously intense, something critics call "its volcanic eruptions of subjectivity." The solemn Andantino, which Robert Bresson has Balthazar die to, goes into F-sharp minor, and is inspired by the German *Lieder*, those romantic solo songs and ballads popularized by poets Heine and Goethe. It's a romance and melancholy that's perfect for a donkey: Bresson chose the right theme tune, the right donkey anthem. The mystical power of Schubert's piano sonata shakes the earth like a braying donkey, but equally has a mercurial tenderness of warm fur, of an innocent "idiot's" stare, of a mountain meadow, of jangling sheep bells, of donkey death. Schubert's piano is the sound of tragic braying, of anybody who lies down to die, alone, in an empty field, after toiling all their lives without reward. It's the sound of us, of our donkey years, of our hopefulness tinged with our hopelessness, of darkness entering the soul, of the beginnings of autumn.

A dog's bark carries across the valley. White light haloes the mountains. They'll soon recede into a stately blackness. Phantom birds sing their final chorus before bedtime. I'm traipsing, a little raggedly, a little wearily, in front of Gribouille, steadily up the shale track, humming to myself, perhaps in A Major. La Chaise-Dieu's Benedictine abbey is there ahead. Its giant twin bell towers dominate, visible from miles below, guiding pillars for travelers, holy beacons that illuminate the way up to the village, a trek I know already, one I have accomplished a few times before.

The abbey is the spiritual hearth of a high-altitude village that's oddly cosmopolitan in its feel, perhaps because of the tourists who attend its summer classical music festival, perhaps because of the village's New Age edge. Inside the abbey, near the west wall, are artistic treasures: sixteenth-century Flemish tapestries and a fifteenth-century unfinished "Dance Macabre" wall fresco, where the naked dead haunt the living, romping against a blood-red backdrop, reminding both lowborn and dignities—popes and cardinals, emperors and kings, knights and merchants, squires and schoolmasters—that before the plague, before war, everyone is equal in death, that the Grim Reaper's scythe will see everybody off someday, each one of us.

A pilgrim with a donkey isn't so uncommon around these parts. Since the twelfth century, pilgrims have set off southeast from here, to Puy-en-Velay, Haute-Loire's chief town. From there, they've headed for Spain, across the Pyrenees and onward to Santiago de Compostela—*St. Jacques de Compostelle*—to the shrine of St. James (Saint Jacques). The apostle spent years preaching in Spain before returning to Jerusalem and martyrdom. After his death, it's said that followers put James's body into a stone boat, which angels and the wind carried beyond the Straits of Gibraltar, up toward Spain's northern Atlantic coast. Then, in A.D. 830, an old hermit, spurred on by a vision, found the spot where James supposedly rested, a marble tomb in Santiago, in Galicia. Once word got out, the pilgrimages began, for millions and millions of Christians, from all over Europe: for sinners seeking penance, for believers paying respects, for the sick needing miracles. And they still come, latter-day pilgrims, along the four ancient routes, departing from Paris, Arles, Vézeley, and Le Puy, on foot, on bikes, and, sometimes, with a donkey, with Balaam's donkey, one that sees angels.

꧂

I wish I believed in miracles. But I don't, really. Nor am I seeking penance. Perhaps I should be. And yet I suppose I'm a sort of pilgrim, one who's traveling to understand, who's here to learn, to learn the forgotten wisdom of the forest, the secret essence of the magic mountain. Gribouille's company helps me understand, lets me find my way. He sees me fumbling sometimes, yet never gripes. He knows we aren't searching a specific end, that we're not embarked on any special quest. It's an everyday venture for us. We're traveling because . . . well, because we're traveling. The world totters, yet beside me he stands firm, offers me solidity, a time and space where there's more time and space.

We're descending a little alleyway near the village square, with its fountain and café and grocery store and bakery all dwarfed by the abbey. Our shadows, stiff in the mountain coolness, shuffle down the slope, search for *Le Clos de l'Atre*—for the cozy pew before the fireplace. It's a fourteenth-century stone building, four stories high, with tanned wooden shutters, restored outside and almost wholly renovated inside. An impressive chimney is the dining room's centerpiece; old oak beams prop up the five-room *Chambres d'Hôtes,* Pascal and Bernadette's family enterprise; I'll eat with them later, around their *table d'hôte,* with a crew of yoga enthusiasts, there for a week's intensive exercise and recharging. We'll have plenty to talk about over supper.

Before I do anything, I need to get Gribouille snug for the night. I'm walking him to a tiny field, a bit too tiny for a donkey; he's minus saddlebags, but there's nowhere here to roll. It's crammed with overhanging trees and overgrown with nettles and bramble. I need to watch I don't get stung. There's a bucket of water near the wire fencing, though he doesn't want to drink a drop. I feel bad about abandoning him here: he looks miserable, the poor mite, his white muzzle glowing in the eerie darkness, standing alone next to the tree, downcast, in a strange place, wondering what to do next. He's even stopped eating. I feel lonely myself, wandering back to my bivouac, an existential chill that sometimes hits travelers after a while on the road. Later that night, cheered by the meal, by a salad made with fried streaky bacon, by the wine and convivial company, as I dozed off on my single bed, a bit tipsy, I heard what I thought was a doleful bray, a gentle rattling under the harvest moon. It trotted through the meadow of my dreams. It was Gribouille, of course, bidding me *bonne soirée*, crying a midnight sonnet. I could hear him full of sighs, out of my good ear ...

23

I'M LATE STARTING off this morning. I spent a long time over coffee talking with Pascal, the proprietor of the *chambres d'hôtes*, about his adopted village. He's a cultured man who once did the urban thing in Grenoble, who cites Mallarmé's poetry from memory, and who now does okay as a *néo-rural*, welcoming visitors to an unexpectedly diverse mountain community. The old folk, the *paysannat*, who've been here forever and who eke out a modest existence from the land, and new arrivals like Pascal hit it off pretty much fine. They share, after all, the same project: keeping the village alive; and both parties need one another.

Newer denizens made a choice to come, to do something different, to exist alternatively, marginally somehow, downsized. The perks are lower-cost living, cheap properties, properties usually in need of rehab; but it's bleak in winter, reputedly one of the coldest areas of France, and isolated; and there's endless steady work to keep life afloat, to stop it from freezing up.

It's twenty minutes before Gribouille and I find real open road, quiet countryside again. We're following a route that'll take us to a lake in a forest. We're moving downhill and it's plain sailing for a while. The trail is stony but stable. Gribouille seems content to walk, to advance with measured steps. It's just as well that he never asks me where we're going. Often I'm not sure myself. He walks alongside me, never querying why. Perhaps he knows why. I suppose I've made a choice similar to Pascal: to live a little marginally, a bit differently. It didn't seem a choice hard to make. Years ago, decades ago, that choice may have been possible in a big city. Not anymore.

The hours have slipped by, drifted away as we've been drifting. The sky has turned ashen and a mist is hovering above the hilltops. A depression is circling in, and a high wind is blowing, fanning stormy air, shaking the trees, whipping up forest debris. It's beginning to rain. The lake is really lapping against the bank and we're getting wet, increasingly chilly; big drops are falling. I can hear them hitting the leather packsaddle, feel them soaking my flannel shirt. We need to find cover under the trees. Nothing to do except wait, stay put, until the rain stops. Gribouille is standing still, meditative, and not much interested in eating anything around here. I'm stroking his fringe, then rubbing lower down his muzzle. We're waiting together, just waiting in the woods. The rain pitter-patters on the canopy and ricochets off the pond. I smell raw earth rising as the downpour eases. Primeval lull returns to the banks of this lakeland prairie.

Gribouille isn't moving, pure and simple. He doesn't like the path beside the water's edge, the one I want to take, the shortest route around the lake. It hugs the curvature of the shoreline, but it's too close to *wetness* for him, too adjacent to the unknown. He's not going along there. No use tugging, getting angry. No alternative but to turn around, to go backward before going forward again, to take him where he's happy to step. Gribouille doesn't let himself get dragged down any old lane, in any old—or new—manner. It's his 8,000-year obstinacy, I guess, faithfully applied, well practiced, you could say. So often, people let themselves be led down paths against their better interests, cajoled somehow, seduced into doing stuff, following because everybody else follows, does likewise, takes that path. It's usually easier to be led and to follow than to take a different route, to stand your ground stubbornly, and go where you want to go, where *you believe is right.*

So often, it's the fastest route that people want to take. They think it's the best, the most direct. Sometimes it is the best. Yet often it gets blocked up with other people and you end up going slow, slower than the slower route. Frequently, it's hard to turn back or take a detour. It's gridlock. Of course, sometimes the stubborn people get it wrong, take different routes that prove dead ends, or become wrong turns with hindsight. God knows, I've made a few of those myself. Perhaps going to America was one wrong turn, a left on red. I don't know. But en route, down these back alleys, strange things have happened, stranger than we imagined, and unknown vistas have been glimpsed, unforeseen encounters taken place, even when you had to turn back—especially when you had to turn back. It often works out because it's what you *really* thought was the right route, the best for you.

It's gone cold again. Nighttime closes in around us. Pascal and I have both opted for another ideal of the Good Life, a dirtier, greener one; a life with a list of chores to keep you busy every day. You have to write them down. They never cease. Nobody delivers pizza to your door. So you need to be organized, prepared, active. That's not always easy if you're isolated or alone. Older folk speak of their own special rural struggle: *lutter contre la solitude*— struggling against solitude. Out here you live in genuine relation with the seasons; you've no choice. I feel cold in winter, *real* cold each morning, and heat in summer—not the reverse, not like in the city, with stifling central heating and freezing air-conditioning. Each day the learning curve is as steep as that hill over there, that blackening mass. And you need to climb it on foot. You start preparing for winter even before summer is done. It's like playing chess: you plan several moves ahead.

❧

I've lost familiarity and security. All that's gone, been flushed down the Hudson River. I'm drifting an ocean away on dry land, without a lifeboat. Not that I really had familiarity anyway. America always felt strange and insecure, always felt *other* somehow. Daily life was easier, cushier than now; yet somehow, too, I had to struggle more, had more threats, especially economic threats. There was a disconnect somewhere. I thought I'd amass new ideas, develop myself, prosper existentially, boost my career, live out my dream. I was lucky, I guess, realizing a dream. Yet no matter how I tried, no matter where I went, I couldn't find my way, couldn't stake out my own corner, feel at home, stay content. In the end, the dream fleeced me of everything, had me throw in the towel with what I'd studied for, worked at for so long. I quit, walked away worse off, dispossessed, yet freer.

With hindsight, I know now the problem was really inside me: *I* was the problem. You see, I'd set such high standards for this dream, held on to them fiercely for thirty years, that now that I had this dream, was living it out, I *absolutely* had to be happy. How could I not be? This was *it*: there was nowhere else to go, no place else to dream of. And for a while I convinced myself that I was happy, that I *needed to be happy*. How could I not be happy? Yet, deep down, I was very unhappy, very lost, but denied it, deluded myself. I was *enslaved;* and part of being free was freeing myself of this dream, and of the ambition of the dream, smashing it, breaking out of it forever, doing something utterly *beyond* the dream. I thought then that I was in control; but I had to admit to myself that I wasn't, that I was out of control, that I was wrong. It was a sense of disappointment that I didn't know how to handle.

Often we set ourselves goals we think will make us

happy, goals we aim for, pursue ardently, believing happiness resides *only* in their attainment. But it's these goals that cause our unhappiness, that condemn us, whether we achieve them or not. They force us down a specific route, with no turning back, no room for detour. Happiness, we believe, lies down this one road only. Henceforth we've little scope for maneuver and a lot of meanwhile to fill. And once we're there, what do we do next? So I've given up now on trying to make my dreams real. I make sure they stay strictly bedtime affairs, modest bedtime affairs. I take comfort from something Jacques Brel sang in *Avec Élé-gance:* "No longer having grand things to dream of / But to listen to a heart that dances / To be desperate / But with elegance." Listening to my heart dance, I daydream instead now, in a place I never dreamed I'd be, where I've been cast by chance, not by volition. Of this place I ask nothing, expect nothing, make no demands. And it expects nothing in return. We sort of get along, together, instinctively, like I get along with Gribouille. Therein lies our tacit agreement, the secret story of our success—our elegance.

24

ANOTHER MORNING, ANOTHER day on planet donkey, tumbling into one another, like in a dream, a daydream. Maybe this is all make-believe, the misty mountain-hop of memory, of remembering what never took place, what has been only imagined, willed outside of history, better than history, a reverie. I'm grooming Gribouille in an enclosure next to a small lumberyard. Giant logs are piled up, whole pine trees. They seem to be piled up. I hear the sound of sawing, of a machine cutting up wood, whirring, and of a tractor chugging on the other side of the trees. Back and forth it goes. There was once a train line running through the yard, probably going to Le Puy. Its tracks are rusted up now, overrun with nettles and weeds, oxidized in the unprofitable air.

Docs anybody still daydream anymore? Are we too busy, too preoccupied to muse, too fearful to keep quiet, to say nothing and just stare, just drift off somewhere? Who still sits quietly, sips their coffee, and stares out the window at life, or stares down at the cosmic cup in front of them, at their entry ticket to the universe? Who still enters into a restful intimacy with himself? Doing nothing nowadays means frustration, boredom, the need for facile stimulation, and TV gives it to you, follows you everywhere: in bars and cafés, in airports and gyms, on billboards, in stores. You either watch it or else you make a call. Everybody is on the phone these days, making noise, fidgeting, lost in action, in speech. Reverie is a dying art, a lost alchemy of the four elements, and of the five senses. Our loss.

Gaston Bachelard, the great philosopher of reverie, saw daydreaming as a sort of rest—*repos*—and a special kind of lyric poetry. Through reverie, Bachelard says, we all become poets, all experience lucid poetic moments. For him, daydreamers "relish the gift of an hour that knows the plenitude of the soul." The sleeping, nighttime dreamer is in the shadow of himself, he says, whereas the daydreamer is fully present, a subject—not an object—of the dream, somebody in the sunshine, no matter what the weather. Bachelard leaves nightmares and nocturnal cold sweats, of things that go bump in the night, of things we repress when awake, to Freud. The night dream is not ours, he says, it's not our possession; its image escapes us. Reverie, on the other hand, is born naturally, "in an awareness without tension." It's an "image that pleases," because we've created it "beyond all responsibility." There's no well-being without reverie, Bachelard thinks, no everyday poetry without reverie's "original peace," without its solitary primal force.

In the 1950s and 1960s, Bachelard made a series of radio broadcasts, of readings, accessible lectures on the poetics of reverie. Since then, they've made it to CD, and I listen to them all the time, drifting off to his singing *bourguignon* accent, to his rhapsodizing chant to "awakened sleepers" and "lucid daydreamers." With his big gray beard, looking like an Old Testament prophet, Bachelard runs to romantic poets and novelists for inspiration, not to psychoanalysts. He prefers the pensive man to the deep sleeper, the person who dozes off in front of the fire, looking at the burning logs, who wanders in the flames, like Balzac's Rastignac from *Études de femmes*, who says he hears the logs talking back; "at these moments," Balzac said, "the heavier the body with sleep, the more agile the mind."

Bachelard wants us to float in the clouds, to daydream in the blue sky, to develop wings and mimic the birds; or swim with the flowing water, bathe in the "milk of the earth," do it while we're meditating next to the brook, or under a tree, or up on a hilltop. Bachelard loves to understand the reveries the elements inspire, reveries of the will and reveries of the earth, of air, water and fire. Yet, if we put our minds to it, we can daydream anywhere, perhaps over a cup of coffee, maybe even at Starbucks ...

Two small worlds of noble sentiment. They size me up, poke out in the morning air. They don't judge. Gribouille's eyes. In these eyes, I see a touching sadness, a grace. Perhaps I'm trying to live out the purity I see in a donkey's eyes, a purity that may not really exist, cannot really exist, has no right to exist in the human world. Bachelard himself muses on the reverie that an animal's eyes can inspire. Ah, did you ever see a hare on an autumn morning, he asks, did you ever see it sprint a few seconds across the silvery frost, then stop in silence, sit on its hind legs, prick up its ears and stare over the misty horizon? "Its gaze seems to confer peace upon the entire universe," Bachelard says. "At this moment, it's a sacred animal, an animal that should be worshiped." Bachelard associates an animal's peace, Gribouille, your peaceful eyes gazing out into this vast verdurous space, with a "world peace," with a "seeing eye looking at the world." If I look into your eyes long enough, into your glassy pond reflecting the sky, I find peace within their calm waters, up in their wavy cumulus isles; and I can transport myself out of this world into the eyes of a world without limit.

Bachelard also tells us how Bérénice, the protagonist of Maurice Barrès's *Le Jardin de Bérénice* (1891), loves to stare into her donkey's eyes, her donkey's resigned eyes, pained beautiful eyes. Bérénice walks with her donkey on the moors, in the Camargue, by the sea, in the salty air, amid the wild white horses and the bulls and the pink flamingos. She finds consolation and solace in these eyes. She looks into them all the time, finds something consistent and reliable there, something meditative, an escape from a world in perpetual turmoil. From time to time, Bérénice embraces her donkey simply for conveying her fraternity.

The novel's narrator, Philippe, worships Bérénice, whom he sees as the bearer of ancient wisdom, as the nemesis of modern madness; he wants to enter Bérénice's garden—*le jardin de Bérénice*—and never leave. The eyes of Bérénice's donkey become little inanimate objects that provoke grand cosmic reverie, grand cosmic daydreaming. Maurice Barrès calls these donkey eyes a "chapel of meditation." They're a place of reverence, of gentle awe, unforgettable eyes. They're the gravest and most reasonable eyes the world has ever seen. In them, there's an animal dignity, a somber patience, a yearning to stay still.

※

Gribouille's eyes shine with tender wonderment, like the wonderment embodied in Balthazar's eyes, the donkey who knows. They're eyes that give only clues, haunting clues. In *Au Hasard Balthazar*, there's an especially haunting scene involving Balthazar's eyes. He's employed as a circus act, as an entertaining donkey that does math before an audience: he's asked to multiply a series of big sums, and duly stamps his hoof a certain number of times to signify the answer. When Balthazar first arrives at the circus, he's dragged around the enclosures, around cages housing other animals. His eyes make contact with other eyes, amid long silent stares—lingering stares that seem to last forever. There's no animosity or pity between the helpless animals. First he's eyeballing a tiger, behind bars; then a polar bear, then a chimpanzee; then, the longest, and most moving, with an elephant, whose beady little eyes grip Balthazar's. We can almost see the latter's water for an instant, before he's dragged away. Each party seems cognizant of their respective fates; each party is communicating in a secret language: it's us humans, they all silently concur, who're the real circus acts; it's us who're really behind bars, in captivity.

Gribouille's eyes stare everywhere. You can't really tell the point of focus, where he's really looking, or if, in fact, he even sees at all. Perhaps his eyes are windows that cast light on his mind. What you find when you look in is really a soul, a window of peace that happens to see, which is also a bodily organ. The look never alters with mood. Donkeys' eyes reveal nothing other than what they are: they remain utterly constant, absolutely calm, reflecting only what's in the eye of the beholder. They're the sole atomic particle a man can see with the naked eye. They comprise vast waves of light shifting around, and tiny particles, minuscule neutrons; the two are interchangeable, waves and particles, light and matter: what you see depends on how you look, depends on what you want to see, on what you imagine you see.

There's another affecting scene with eyes in *Au Hasard Balthazar*. Marie is the teenage girl whose life history reflects Balthazar's. She's known Balthazar since birth, since she baptized the little baby donkey, Balthazar. She played with him in the meadows, hugged him in the barn, rolled over with him in the hay. Gaily they grew up together, came of age. Then Balthazar has to go away, is sold off because Marie's father couldn't afford a donkey anymore. Thereafter Balthazar's childhood ends; he gets variously abused, and so does Marie, whose own melancholic look mimics Balthazar's. Their luckless fates are entwined. Yet, one night, young Marie is barefoot in the garden and collects flowers for Balthazar. She's made him a little headband, a glowing halo, on which she places flowers. Soon he looks like a lily of the valley. She kisses Balthazar's nose tenderly. She sits on a bench opposite him, admiring him sadly, the donkey who stands there saintly, motionless, with his garland. They watch each other in silence. The scene zooms into Balthazar's eyes and endures for five seconds, a cinematic eternity. Then Gérard, the village thug, and his pal crash into the garden, crash the party. They start to kick the hell out of Balthazar, the donkey crucified.

⚜

We're headed down a grassy path now. Suddenly Gribouille veers off into a field. He's spotted something green and yellow. He darts off with awesome power and determination. He's unstoppable. What's attracting him, I wonder? It takes me a while before I realize that he's eating lentils, green lentils growing in a field without any fencing. He's gobbling them with zeal, a local donkey eating a local product. If I leave him here too long, this season's crop will soon disappear. The plants are still young, scruffy-looking little bushes, weedlike. But if you look closely you can see them coming into flower, delicate buds forming, buds that will eventually become the nourishing Green Lentils of Le Puy-en-Velay, one of the region's best-known export crops, and, like great French wine, an "AOC"—"*appellation d'origine contrôlée.*"

This means that the cultivation of these green diamonds doesn't travel: they're *absolutely* specific to the area, to the eighty-eight communes of the AOC zone surrounding Le Puy. The field Gribouille is demolishing must be the northernmost reach of that zone. With the AOC, taste and quality are guaranteed. Only green lentils that come from Le Puy can be called Le Puy Green Lentils! It's that simple, and that radical, in an epoch when food comes from everywhere, and nowhere, and when people couldn't tell if a tomato or a leek is a winter or summer vegetable. The AOC means no fertilizers and a respect for natural cycles. The Velay's microclimate and its volcanic soil play a crucial role here. There's lots of sunshine each year— this isn't the warmest spot in France, but it's one of the sunniest—and before the lentils are harvested they must reach an accumulated temperature of 930 degrees Celsius. Around here, that takes between 120 and 150 days. Perfect for lentils.

Connoisseurs say these lentils are really a "beefsteak in plant form," though better for your waistline and cholesterol level. They're so easy to prepare, and so tasty, just boil them for twenty minutes in salty water, till they soften—but make sure they don't overcook, don't become too mushy. Oh, and what meals you can have. Gribouille already knows! Mixed with garlic, olive oil, and wine vinegar, a teaspoon of mustard, or with bacon and ham if you prefer, washed down with an earthy, full-bodied wine like a Cahors . . . one of the great pleasures in life. I'll never forget the first time I ate them, late one night, at Champot, after a long day walking; and with local potatoes, *ratte* potatoes, plastered in garlic. It was reclamation of the senses, perhaps the opening of new ones, a new vista of sensuality, finding taste buds I never knew I had. Pure simplicity in a complex life.

I really have to drag Gribouille away. He's gotten all the vitamins and pulses he needs for today, and for this week, I'd say. But we should spare the crop and keep moving on. The strange thing is that when I stop for lunch, stop to eat, he never seems to want to partake. It's often the only moment of the day when he doesn't eat anything, when he just stands there and watches me, sticking his muzzle into my affairs. The weather seems to have changed for the worse, and it's chilly. We've stopped next to a sleepy spot under a few willow trees, trying to find protection from a breeze with a bite in it. I'm sitting on the grass and Gribouille roams freely near the stream. He's content to wander around a bit, to stare out aimlessly, to stare into my eyes.

25

I'VE ALWAYS BEEN aware of my own beady, weak eyes. They look more like a mole's than a donkey's. Since I was very young, these eyes have been bad. My mother reckoned it was due to the fall I'd had, after I banged my head on the fireplace, when I was very young, not long after I'd started to walk. Thereafter a squint developed in my right eye. One day my mother saw my right eye wandering off track, someplace where an eye shouldn't have been wandering. Soon glasses were prescribed, and, as I grew older, a kind of disability and torture began.

But there were advantages. After all, I got to make trips to the eye hospital with my mother. These trips were the thrill of my life; I'll never forget them, even though they're gone forever and I know it and it saddens me. But I can always conjure up the images of those journeys with my mother, going into town every couple of months to the eye hospital. I remember going there and squeezing her hand as we'd walk across Exchange Flags near the Town Hall. All the buildings seemed so big, which I guess they would for the average kid; everything seemed so bustling and exciting and new and a little scary. It was the mid-1960s, before Liverpool began to decline, before people began to leave, before the buildings became shabby and forgotten. For me, it was the greatest place on earth and it was such a big adventure going there.

We had a set routine during the years I went for an eye checkup. In the hospital we'd have to go up a winding staircase where the doctor would have this machine that I had to put my chin on and look at pictures of all kinds of animals: horses, cats and dogs and rabbits, and donkeys. Of course there were donkeys. I had to move a lever to try to place each animal into a cage, or take them out of their cages, or line each animal up. I didn't know what this was all about at the time. All I knew was that it was a whole lot of fun. My mother would be there, too, encouraging me and laughing at her son whose eyesight was poor and who had these thick-lens glasses. Maybe she guessed I was afraid that I might have to stay in hospital for an operation, stay in for a while. But the real treat always came afterward, when my mother took me out for lunch.

We'd always stop off at the Indian restaurant above "Hobbies," a kids' toy shop I loved, long disappeared, along with the Indian restaurant. My mother used to let me have a chicken curry. As ever, she knew it would be way too hot. I don't know why I had it, because every time she'd have to ask for more water to cool my mouth. We'd laugh about it as I'd sweat and suffer, gasping for air and fanning my mouth. I know now that the curry probably wasn't very good. But right then and there, it was the best curry in the world.

All those memories of the eye hospital came flooding back the day I saw my mother die, years and years later, when I was an adult, a lost adult. She was barely awake when she greeted my presence at her bedside. She'd been immobile for nearly two months already. Her eyes were sunken, withdrawn, her complexion yellowing; she had this little tuft of hair left, all gray and ruffled on a skull that peeked out of the sheets, receding into the bed, into nothingness, vanishing in front of my eyes, those eyes that once saw animals. She had "borne him in her arms and in her heart," said Stephen Dedalus in *Ulysses*. "But for her the race of the world would have trampled him un- derfoot, a squashed boneless snail. She had loved his weak watery blood drained from her own."

She reached out her hand very frailly, which I held. Tears flooded down my face. Her voice by then was weak and croaky. She began to stroke my hand, maybe not even knowing she was stroking it. I told her I wanted to cry because I hadn't done enough before. She told me to go ahead and said what a good baby I'd been because I wasn't a crier, not like my elder sister, she said, who'd cried all the time. No, I was a good baby. I said I was still a good baby and asked her if she remembered the times we used to go into Liverpool city center when I was about five or six, to the eye hospital. These trips are the fondest images of my childhood, perhaps of my entire life. I'll always see them, even if I go blind.

26

WHEN I OPENED my eyes that morning, another student morning in that dingy college room, everything was strange. As I moved my head to the right and left, up and down, things turned black, the lights somehow went out in my left eye. Weird black blobs obstructed my vision. They seemed black, anyway, but they could've been green, dark green. I wasn't sure. Sort of dark-greeny-black blobs then. They slushed around as I slushed around: a vivid psychedelic dance bopped away. I closed one eye, opened it again. Still the blobs floated, a viscous membrane, an amoeba visible only to me.

In front of a mirror I stared into my eyes, deeply, with intent, searching for evidence, a sign. Nothing. Nothing within, within those dark unrevealing eyes, neither in the right nor the left. Too many lines of words, black and white spaces, read. Lamp-lit silence. I had pained to see, to know, to understand, in the little bookish corner I'd occupied. I'd made it to Oxford, on a scholarship, worked myself silly, and now, finally, I'd burned my eyes out, ruined them forever. I panicked once outdoors, trembled as I walked to the hospital emergency unit. Ironically, I lived practically next door to the hospital, it was that close, along Walton Street. The doctor shocked me with her diagnosis: Rhegmatogenous retinal detachment and vitreous hemorrhage.

I'd have to go for eye surgery, to repair that retina, to glue it back where it belonged; I'd have to be admitted *this afternoon*. Next thing I knew I was stretched out on a bed, fully clothed, in a room all to myself. The doctors were curious, perplexed. It, I, was an enigma. Though it was more "It." My eye became the object, the subject of intrigue; the I, which is to say me, was incidental. They poked and shined beams into my face, bright, bright lights, from all angles, at all times, probing deep into the rear of my eyeball, peeping at that fragile filmic skin, now damaged, torn, ripped off its socket, mangled through wear and tear. My pupils were dilated. All I could see was a dense white fog.

I'd slept very uneasily in that strange bed, with unfamiliar smells, unfamiliar noises. When I dropped off, I dreamed mad, raving things, feverish, hallucinogenic nightmares. Eye patches, blindness, white sticks, a knife cutting open my eye, seeing my own blood pouring before me, dripping ... No more studying, no reading or writing. And what if the surgery went wrong, hideously wrong? It did sometimes. It did often. I'd be alone in old age, invalid and blind, immobile and poverty-stricken, with nobody left to help me. I was terrified, waking up in a delirious frenzy, sweating, confused. The wall was on the wrong side, the bed was somehow out of place. For a split second I wondered where I was. Then I remembered. Next time I opened my eyes, it was morning. The sun rushed in, and my fears seemed allayed for a while.

I'd have to have an operation. No, I wouldn't. Yes, I probably would. Then somebody said the prognosis was more cheery but more uncertain, potentially more problematical. It wasn't a detachment at all. There'd be no surgery, not for a while anyway, perhaps never. A schisis cavity, just a hole, a big hole, but very peripheral for now, maybe always so. We can only hope. There's a point of demarcation, between the bit still glued on, the good bit, the seeing bit, and the unglued part, the unseeing bit, the bit where there's going to be permanent shadow. That was the good news. It was in both eyes, apparently. Normal, they said, but more advanced in the left. It could be congenital, might even be hereditary. Usually it happened in older people; odd for somebody so young—so relatively young. If it plays up again, come back. There might be trouble if it rips more. We could try to repair it with lasers. We'll see. Don't think about a career in boxing . . .

The seeing eye guards its window on the world for another day. I remember my father coming down from Liverpool, to check if all was okay. We went for a long walk together later that day, after my discharge. We talked about nothing. Sometimes neither of us said anything. The silences were comfortable and brimmed with meaning. It was enough just to look, to stroll, to imbibe an Oxford spring afternoon. As dusk fell, we ended up in Christ Church Meadow. I no longer remember how or why. It was a beautiful evening, with a starlit orange sky, and an atmosphere of woody freshness, of warm dampness underfoot. A layer of mist hovered over the moor. Somehow, we got locked in, missed the closing of the gates, giant gates, fortified with speared railings, twenty-foot tall.

Somehow, we had to ascend them; we inched our way upward. Somehow, Father made it over, red-faced, grunting, in good spirits. We could climb anything that night. And afterward, a well-earned pint of bitter, in the King's Arms: nectar. A brew that out-brewed all brews. We drank and conversed and mingled like never before, perhaps like never again. Father and son conjoined in adulthood. Soon dad began his familiar seaman's tales, of matches from Chile, of Montreal in the fifties, of drinking gallons of evaporated milk, of bars and hoodlums. He drank evaporated milk by the bucketful, he said. I'd heard it a million times already, though that night was happy to hear it again. And he even found a Canadian who knew those bars he'd frequented, beside us, drinking in the King's Arms. Later, father and son tottered home, like Bloom and Stephen exiting Bella Cohen's; the former took the single bed, snoring away moments later like a contented warthog. The latter slept on the floor and was immediately overcome with a blissful nothingness, a blissful seeing nothingness . . .

※

I'm glad I'm outside in the fresh air, in this damp morning in the Auvergne, still seeing, still standing, still wandering. I wonder what it would be like not to see: I close my eyes sometimes and walk, trying merely to listen and smell. I feel Gribouille's warm fur, hear him breathing and sighing. He can always lead me onward, be my guide, my seeing eye, my seeing eye looking at the world. If I was blind I'd still be able to smell and hear, at least out of one ear, and rub my donkey when I wanted, retain tactile sense. That wouldn't be so bad, would it? I'd had a brush with darkness. But thinking about it has me breathe a breath of relief today, affirm a life-affirming freshness, despite the weather outside. In fact, there's a certain ecstasy to my step, to our step.

I seem to be acutely aware of detail, of color, of contrast, of light and shadow, of moods and postures and smiles. We've just encountered a couple of men with a sheep dog, out collecting mushrooms, hunting for *cèpes*, and I smiled and chatted. One mushroom man told me he has his own donkey; he gave Gribouille's fringe a brisk rub in passing, before walking off with his giant bag of goodies, the season's first. Yes, I seem to be seeing everything with clarity this morning, a relieved morning, a wondrous morning, like all mornings. How precious life is, how vulnerable we all are, like donkeys: finite, wounded creatures. I'm all right now, safe for the time being, accompanied. It's life and life only.

27

WE'RE IN THE heart of a village, a medieval gem, in a square that's really like a large enclosed courtyard, surrounded on all sides by narrow three-story shuttered houses. Everything is turned inward and hangs together as a interrelated whole, facing the public square; buildings relate to one another, despite the different architectural forms, and nothing is left out, separated or segregated from anything else, pushed out in the cold. You get the impression that sixteenth-century planners were savvier than their modern counterparts about how to build a real community, about how to let it grow organically.

We're next to a fountain; again Gribouille doesn't want to drink. Even when donkeys are thirsty and need water, they'll never drink dirty water. The water in the old fountain looks pretty clean to me. But it's an unfamiliar trough for Gribouille, and so he's characteristically cautious. I don't worry about him not drinking; I know donkeys have lower water requirements than any other animal, apart from camels. They can go without water for three days without suffering any harm. In hot climates, donkeys can still work even when they're dehydrated. In fact, they can withstand up to a 25% weight loss due to dehydration and still recover afterward, when water becomes available again. Their daily requirement depends upon environment (like availability of moist greenery), air humidity levels, ambient temperature, and intensity of any work they're performing. It's generally agreed that between five and nine gallons of water a day is an acceptable benchmark for donkeys to drink, and this should be offered at least once a day to ensure good digestive functioning. And it shouldn't be too cold either, particularly if it's summer, especially if they're still hot from working.

Donkeys have special digestive systems that break down even the most indigestible food; from this food they can extract and conserve as much moisture as possible. So when Gribouille eats his leafy greens, he's sort of drinking, too. No surprises there, given that donkeys hail from the desert and evolved because they could withstand long treks searching for sparse vegetation and fresh water. This digestive system helped them survive dry, harsh environments; such a digestive system likewise evolved *because of* such dryness and became adept at dealing with drought and dry seasons. That a donkey is equipped with extremely mobile lips and a narrow muzzle means they can graze and browse with extreme sensitivity, scooping up the best *quality* vegetation when the overall *quantity* of vegetation is limited. And in the wild, the need to track down this food and drink, always kept donkeys lean and alert, constantly on the move. For domesticated donkeys, where high-quality food and drink is generally abundant, and where perimeter fencing reduces a donkey's ability to roam freely, the big dilemma, like the big dilemma for humans, is lack of exercise and overfeeding, especially eating food with poor roughage and mineral content.

We're a long way from any desert now, a long way from Gribouille's roots, from an environment where water is worth its weight in gold, where "the smallest drop," said Antoine de Saint-Exupéry, "extracts from the sand the green spark of a blade of grass." Five or six kids on bikes, about ten years old, bright-faced, healthy looking, have gathered around us near the fountain. They start quizzing me about Gribouille. They're showing real curiosity about my companion. These kids are outdoors most of the day in summer. They're all lined up opposite us, sitting on their saddles; none can resist patting him. I've seen Gribouille in these situations before: he secretly laps up the attention, and stands there taking it calmly, enjoying the caressing. What's his name? How old is he? Where have we come from? From very far? Oh, that's a long way away, isn't it. They're inquisitive about my friend and about me. Kids can instinctively tell you're not from these parts; you can see it in their eyes, in the way they twinkle, the way they sense strangeness, otherness. Kids can ride their bikes around here in relative safety because there aren't megahighways to cross or monster roads to navigate. The village was built for pedestrians.

I'd like to stay and linger more, because there's a summer market this evening, *un marché du soir,* in the same square. Local producers will sell their modest wares from little stalls: fruit and vegetables, lentils and charcuterie, pottery and woodwork, plants and paintings. There'll be food and other things going on, like dancing and music and drinking, always drinking, harmless fun, often corny kinds of fun. One of the nice things locals have inherited from their Middle Age forebears is an ability to *laugh,* to party, to have a big fête in summer. You can glimpse the way it used to be done in classic French texts of that period, like Rabelais's *Gargantua and Pantagruel,* with its great feasts of food and drink, rambunctious reveling and bawdy humor, celebrating life and the fruits of nature. These fêtes were, and still are, sorts of public catharses, popular safety values releasing everyday passions, keeping the community together and alive despite the difficulties they face. But I've got to find my lodgings for tonight, got to keep moving, can't stay; I've got a ways to go yet.

※

The sun is starting to dip behind me, disappearing increasingly earlier now, feeling weaker by the day. I'm holding the lead rope and stroking Gribouille's head, along his crest. We're doing well down a narrow, unused path, almost knee-deep in grass, surrounded by flat fields of corn. In a few weeks, the crop will be hacked down and the corn ground into winter cattle feed. The track is pleasantly soft for Gribouille. Every so often he'll swoop down and have his green fill. We pass a semiderelict house, with a crumbling wall around it and a rusty metal gate with a sign attached: À VENDRE—For Sale. There's a tractor working somewhere and the gentle, consistent pulse of insects; an early evening peace descends, a comforting, ordinary peace. Only the sky is exceptional: crinkled crimson folds itself around the horizon, with autumnal gray twists, and a moon not quite full, near enough to touch.

I look out toward that horizon, try to appropriate it; I look at the fields and the trees and the hills, the endless rolling, breathing countryside I will as my own, declare mine. I look at Gribouille, the great hermetic waddler, head down, saddlebags dangling either side, and think of myself, here, now, like this, in my solitude, in my self-chosen exile, on the move, fleeing. I think of Stevenson, whose presence isn't far away, who understood this lightsome spirit: "For my part," he said of his voyage in the Cévennes, "I travel not to go anywhere, but to go. The great affair is to move; to feel the needs and hitches of our life more nearly; to come down off this feather-bed of civilization, and find the globe granite underfoot and strewn with cutting flints." I breathe in the west wind and reach out for the moon.

That evening I'm with Régis and Suzette in their *Chambres d'Hôtes*, and another couple Anne and Eric with their young, happy family, three lovely kids, all out to enjoy an Auvergne vacation. They're far from their Brittany home. Gribouille has company tonight, in a field with two other donkeys, young grays, *petits* fellas, whom he sniffed and seemed happy to be alongside. Régis expertly whisked him off upon our arrival. I followed to ensure he'd be okay, that he'd have access to fresh water in a clean container. The enclosure had a little bolted wooden gate surrounded by barbed wire. Not ideal, perhaps, but there's sufficient space.

Over dinner Régis tells us he used to be a farmer. But now he works for an organization specializing in artificial insemination, mainly artificial insemination of dairy cows. Cows are impregnated with sperm from bulls, he explains, for improved milk production and for better and more abundant cheese. This happens with sheep and goats, too, he says, where genetic semen from superior sires and bucks is used to breed higher-quality flocks, again for their milk, again for cheese. It's an issue Régis is keen to explain as we wolf down local pork from his brother-in-law's butcher's store, beautifully cooked by Suzette, with masses of potatoes cooked in meat fat.

He's filling our glasses and we're all slurping down the red wine. He's an interesting character, self-educated, reads a lot, did military service in Algeria, and was mayor of the village for years and years. He's ardent about politics, at every scale, and talks about the "French crisis," about the presidential elections in France, and the bankruptcy of every candidate. "There's a lot of anxiety," he says. I tell him I was once into politics, followed it closely, though not anymore. It bores me now, detracts from the nicer, more important things in life, like literature and art, and love. Everybody concurs that the world isn't in good shape. But we're all too merry tonight to let that bother us.

28

THERE'S SOMETHING TREMENDOUSLY democratic about a donkey's tail. It sounds a bit mad to say that, I know, but there is, there really is. I'm watching Gribouille's now, swishing about to shoo away the flies. It's the perfect instrument for getting rid of flies. He's decided to sit down today, to take a rest in a little ray of sunshine during our midmorning break. You can hear the dull thump sometimes, when his tail whips against the earth. Thump. There it goes again. I'm sitting on a tree trunk that's fallen down, browsing through *Le Monde*, the French daily. Pine trees surround us; we're in a clearing, and the ground is soft and open and Gribouille's packsaddle is off. When you remove the packsaddle, you're obliged to take off the elastic strap that goes around a donkey's *derrière*, that fits under their tail. You need to move the tail, pick it up to flick the strap over. The tail feels gristly near the top, around the dock, near where it joins the rump: it feels like thick rope.

A donkey's tail is different from a horse's: less proud, less flamboyant, more disheveled like a cow's, more Zen-like in its rumpled simplicity, with its short body hair and tuft at the end. It's somehow just *there*: a frayed, everyday rudder, without pretense. There's a Haitian proverb that frowns on fancy airs and graces and runs something like this: "The donkey sweats so the horse can be decorated with lace." I think that tells us something about the difference in their tails. There's a sort of popular wisdom to a donkey's tail, nothing fancy, unlike a horse's; that's what I mean about it being democratic. Pinning the tail on a donkey, giving it a populist spin, and under a democratic banner, was something Andrew Jackson did when he ran for the U.S. presidency in 1828. "Let the people rule!" said Jackson. "What a jackass," opponents called him, on account of his perceived stubbornness. Yet Jackson turned nasty name-calling into political folklore; the donkey epithet stuck and Jackson worked it to his own advantage, mobilizing donkey campaign posters, with a tail-wagging manifesto, and later defeated the aristocratic John Quincy Adams.

A few years later, in 1830, when Jackson vetoed the rechartering of the National Bank, a pillorying cartoon caricatured the old jackass; Jackson's braying head and ruffled tail appears on a dancing donkey's body, down on the farm, among the chickens (branch banks) and frothing dogs (chambers of commerce). Curiously, too, in 1837, after Jackson retired, he became the brunt of another donkey lampoon: still believing himself the Democratic Party's spiritual godfather, he was pictured as a latter-day Balaam, blindly trying to get his donkey (the American people) to go where he wanted, against its will. Since then the donkey has stuck as the Democrats' unofficial pet logo (and the elephant the Republican's). But enlightened people everywhere know how Balaam's donkey will always wag its tail to another beat, will always somehow swish above and beyond politics.

Indeed, if you watch a donkey's tail wagging for long enough, you'll recognize something magisterial as well as populist, perhaps even Beethovenian: this tail shifts around like a great maestro's baton conducting a symphony, dancing through the air, orchestrating its own musical soundtrack. Oftentimes that tail seems to function in unison with those ears, with those antennae: donkeys flap around their ears, shoo away the flies near their head, while they swat with their tail, rid themselves of pests near their rear end. That said, I've never seen a donkey's tail kill a single fly. Their tail is more a deterrent, a hairy peacekeeping force.

In *Au Hasard Balthazar*, Gérard set Balthazar's tail ablaze. He thought this was one way to get to his donkey, to punish him. He's riding his moped alongside Balthazar, holding a chain that's attached to the donkey's halter.

Suddenly, Balthazar stops; he's carrying two large panniers either side of him, both full of baguettes. But he's
not happy being dragged along at Gérard's motorized
pace. Gérard dismounts and starts to push Balthazar's
rump. Nothing. Balthazar doesn't budge an inch. He's
rock-solid and won't move. Then Gérard begins kicking
his backside. Again, nothing. The camera pans to Balthazar as Gérard strikes Balthazar with his fist, really whacks
him. The donkey shows absolutely no emotion. So many
sticks have been broken on his back that their feeble cudgeling leaves him unconcerned. But then Gérard rips out
a page of the newspaper he's got, rolls it up and with a
piece of string ties it to Balthazar's tail. Then he sets the
newspaper alight. Moments later Balthazar runs off, kicking up his back legs, whipping around his tail as the
flames blaze. Gérard reclaims Balthazar standing in a field,
with his head facing some bushes. Schubert's piano sonata begins to play, highlighting Gérard's absurdly destructive behavior and the pity we see in Balthazar's eyes;
pity not for himself, but for Gérard, and for us.

❧

I wonder if you agree, Gribouille, with what Old Benjamin
said in *Animal Farm*: that God had given him a tail to keep
the flies off but he'd sooner have had no tail and no flies?
Gribouille is upright now, with his muzzle in the grass,
foraging rather eating; his tail is still swishing about,
swishing like an impressionist's paintbrush, with rapid,
confident strokes, across an imaginary canvas. Perhaps
you know, Gribouille, of the famous donkey artist Lolo,

157

alias Boronali, and the tale of a donkey's tail, of how it became the talk of the town, the star of Paris's art salons, the legendary artist-in-residence at the Lapin Agile? A lot of people think the mascot of this famous *fin-de-siècle* Montmartre tavern was a rabbit, the eponymous rabbit nimbly avoiding the copper cooking pot; the said rabbit's portrait still adorns the Lapin Agile's wall, a mural visible at the crossroads of the rue des Saules and rue Saint-Vincent on the Butte Montmartre, not far from the Sacré-Coeur.

Yet Lolo was its real star, a chocolate-colored donkey about the size of Toulouse-Lautrec, another Lapin habitué. For years, Lolo sat in the inn under a painting: Picasso's *Au Lapin Agile*, which hung frameless on a wall in the main salon. In 1905, Picasso had given it to Frédéric Gérard, the Lapin's patron and Lolo's owner, and in the picture "Frédé" is seen playing his guitar while Picasso, in a harlequin-patterned sweater, sits drinking wine. (In 1912, Frédé sold the picture for next to nothing—for *"une bouchée de pain"*—practically giving it away; in 1989, Sotheby's auctioned it for $41 million, and today it's hung where no donkeys are allowed to sit: in New York's Metropolitan Museum of Art.)

All the Lapin's esteemed clientele knew Lolo: not just Picasso, but other artists like Modigliani and Maurice Utrillo, Max Jacob and Georges Braque; and writers and poets like Alfred Jarry and Guillaume Apollinaire, Francis Carco and Pierre Mac Orlan. Frédé himself was a poetic presence, with a long white beard, red headscarf, and wooden clogs, wandering around the Butte's cobbled streets with

Lolo in tow, playing either guitar or flute, always with an ear out for what went on. People said Frédé looked like a cross between an Alaskan trapper and Robinson Crusoe after years and years of shipwreck. Frédé often supplemented his Lapin income by selling fish from Lolo's panniers. Frédé apparently talked little; but when he did, he sounded like a Homeric sage: "I love donkeys," he'd once said, "because they're horses who haven't succeeded." Lolo never left Frédé's side, and his bray was just as familiar to the *montmartrois* as the bells of Notre Dame.

It was one evening at the Lapin, one evening in March 1910, that Lolo's tail swished some masterstrokes. It had all started as a practical joke, as a parody, orchestrated by another inn regular, Roland Dorgelès, a journalist and novelist. Dorgelès gives a lively rendering of Lolo's big night in a memoir called *Bouquet de Bohème* (1947). For a while, Dorgelès had despaired about artistic fashion, about the charlatans in its midst, about the state of so-called "modern art." He didn't much like cubism either. Everybody professed to be an artist, a painter, yet few really were. Then an idea struck to mock the "isms" of the day: Dorgelès would coin a new one: "excessivism," and Lolo would become its *chef d'école*, the leader of this new school of "Futurism." "Excess in art is a force," joked Dorgelès. "The sun is never too ardent, the sky never too green, the sea never too red. The place of genius is to dazzle!"

But Lolo couldn't be plain old Lolo; he needed another name, and he needed to be Italian, like all the other "Futurists": Boronali! Boronali was an anagram of Aliboron, and Aliboron was the name of a donkey in a Jean de la Fontaine fable. The famed seventeenth-century fabler, a sort of French Aesop, though often a lot nicer to donkeys, has Aliboron figure in a 1668 tale of *The Thieves and the Donkey*: "A donkey is," wrote la Fontaine there, "by interpretation, / some province poor, or prostrate nation. / The thieves are princes of this and that. / On spoils and plunder prone to fat, / As those of Austria, Turkey, Hungary, / (Instead of two, I have quoted three—Enough of such commodity.) / These powers engaged in war all, / Some fourth thief stops the quarrel, / According all to one key, / By riding off the donkey."

So that March evening, with Frédé standing by, a blank canvas was set up on an easel at the Lapin and Joachim-Raphael Boronali was beckoned to reverse toward it. Dorgelès and sidekick André Warnod attached a paintbrush to Lolo's tail; and, after they dipped the brush into oil paint, Lolo's tail went to and fro across the canvas. From time to time the paintbrush was replaced. After enough blue was daubed, it was switched for red; after that, green. So it went. Sufficient provisions stood by: "I had only to put a carrot under his nose," said Dorgelès, "in order that he'd manifest pure asinine joy, and he'd resume the smearing with his tail." In a bit over an hour, with a large group gathering, "Lolo gobbled down a cabbage, a leek, some endives, a lettuce, radishes, spinach, celery . . ." But the result was a dazzling impressionist canvas, *Coucher de soleil sur l'Adriatique* ("Sunset on the Adriatic"), full of flowing pinks and radiant marine blues, a stunning debut effort.

Six days later, the Salon des Indépendants opened its doors, where artists display their works, reach out to audiences, and try to get discovered. *Coucher de soleil sur l'Adriatique* drew large crowds eager to see the chef d'oeuvre of *le chef d'école* of excessivism. " 'Where's the sea?' one woman quizzed her husband. 'Down there, of course.' 'But it's all red!' 'So what? I'm telling you he's a futurist . . .' " The press soon picked up on the Boronali affair. One art journal said there was "an excess of personality" in the canvas; another that it had "a temperament of a confused colorist"; others spoke of a "precocious mastery." The critics, evidently, were divided. Then Dorgelès came clean to the newspaper *Le Matin,* and the gag was out of the bag: Boronali was a donkey! *Coucher* was painted with a donkey's tail!

Still, this only added to the notoriety of the painting, and to Lolo the artist. People started to flock to the Lapin, made pilgrimages to glimpse Frédé's donkey, left bouquets, sent well-wishing cards; some artists looked at Lolo with envy, since he was now more famous than they'd ever be. Journalists published portraits of Lolo; yet, as ever with a donkey, "he stayed modest." "If all our mates showed off as little as him," Frédé observed, "we'd all be tranquil around here." Eventually, the painting sold for the tidy sum of 400 francs at a time when your average Raoul Dufy went for a couple of sous. Over the years, Lolo's glory became even grander, not just as an animal savant but as a legendary artist in his own right. Thus, in the influential *Dictionnaire des peintres* of Bénézit, you find: "Boronali, J.-R., painter born Gênes in the 19th century. (Italian School.)"

29

YET THE TALE of Lolo's tail has a sad end. During the First World War, Lolo retired to the village of Saint-Cyr-sur-Morin, these days an hour's train ride from Paris's Gare de l'Est. There, he could graze in peace on luscious grass alongside the neighborhood kingfishers, near the willow-banked Petit Morin River, not far from the house of one of France's greatest twentieth-century writers, Pierre Mac Orlan, Frédé's son-in-law. Frédé loved the calm of Saint-Cyr, and he had a little *maisonnette* in one of its hamlets, Armenats. Soon, for many *montmartrois* fleeing ever-congested and price-inflated Paris, Saint-Cyr became a fresh-air sanctuary, a Montmartre-on-the-river. They'd gather a five-minute stroll around the corner from chez Mac Orlan, over a humpbacked bridge, at the L'Oeuf Dur tavern—"The Hardboiled Egg"—the Lapin Agile's home away from home.

After his Saint-Cyr sojourns, each time Frédé returned to Paris, Lolo, also longing to return, brayed plaintively. He missed the guys and gals of the Butte, the flea-bitten cabarets, the everyday sentimentality, his promenades with Frédé along ragamuffin back streets. Perhaps, too, he missed his glory days as Boronali in front of the easel? We know donkeys don't like to be alone, that they mourn and grieve over things lost, loved ones, familiar sights and sounds. Indeed, Lolo never seemed to adjust to the country air, never seemed to accept his fresh-air tonic, and, one day, they found the poor old donkey floating in the Morin.

Had he accidentally drowned? Or had he, as some speculated, thrown himself in? A donkey suicide? Is such a thing possible, conceivable? It's rumored that after the prophet Muhammad's death, out of sadness, the donkey Ya'foor threw himself down a deep well, thereby undermining his entry to Muslim Paradise. So perhaps it could happen. Dorgelès, for one, believed Lolo had committed suicide—like other troubled artists, he'd said; and, to a certain degree, Dorgelès held himself responsible: it was he, after all, who'd turned a happy donkey into a tormented celebrity. Had Lolo, under Boronali's banner, yielded to a common anthropomorphism, fallen foul of conceited human ways?

※

It was freezing the day I stood on that humpbacked bridge at Saint-Cyr. I didn't see any kingfishers, or any donkeys. But I could imagine Lolo down there, in summer, munching under the willows. The whole of the Seine-et-Marne department glowed in luminescent white, after the previous day's carpeting. There wasn't a soul about. I trampled through the snow, listening to the wind whistle between the trees, feeling its icy chill blow off the Petit Morin.

Soon I approached a collection of five or six houses, two-storied, quaint, all with pink-colored walls made from local gypsum, all with light-blue doors and shutters. They looked onto an open courtyard, a spacious public lawn. You could visualize old cronies playing *boules* on it. In the left-hand corner, beside a big barn door, is the Oeuf Dur's old mural, fading but still palpable, almost Art Nouveau in style. The "hard-boiled egg" pops out in exaggerated proportions, held by an ethereal young nymph, whose gaiety and flamboyance is unashamed, just as the inn's had been, young at heart despite its aging years, now pensioned off.

I was there to experience the world of Pierre Mac Orlan, to smell and touch his slightly foxed universe, which I thought had something important to teach me. The Oeuf Dur was near enough for Mac Orlan to walk to in carpet slippers, to sneak out his back door, to meet pops-in-law Frédé and a few pals from Montmartre. He could smoke his pipe and watch Lolo swish that tail. I remember swishing my own tail, Gribouille, trying to stay warm, searching under a cold light for warming remnants of this bygone age, for a sentimental education no longer found in latter-day curriculums.

For clues, I went to the Musée des Pays de Seine-et-Marne, not far away, which pays homage to Pierre Mac Orlan. All sorts of paraphernalia were there, all sorts of documents, original manuscripts, first-edition books, treasures left open at key pages, records and videos, photos from the Lapin Agile; one has Frédé next to Lolo, both in furtive mode, both poking their heads out of the doorway, suspiciously, on the lookout for trouble; Frédé is feeding Lolo something, perhaps a carrot. I was touched by its innocence: the last of an innocent generation.

One slender book in the display cabinet impressed me a lot, all sixty pages of it: *Petit Manuel du Parfait Aventurier* (1920)—Little Handbook of the Perfect Adventurer. "It's necessary to establish, as a law," Mac Orlan said, "that adventure doesn't exist. It's only in the imagination of those who pursue it and is effaced when you believe you've found it; and when you hold it, it's not worth looking at." Mac Orlan underscored the importance of adventure in the mind, of adventure we find in reverie, in meditative thinking, in apparently useless daydream. He isn't fond of high-tech adventures. Too explosive, he says, too chemical, too noisy; they can't retain people's interest terribly long. Participants have to keep moving on, have to hear louder bangs, do riskier jumps, from greater heights, make ever more hazardous expeditions, up peaks, across deserts, through treacherous jungles, over virgin lands, you name it. It's all distraction, all leisure, getting away from everything, *forgetting*, at least for a day, maybe for a week. A vacation, if you're lucky.

And yet there exist other kinds of adventures and other kinds of adventurers: people less active, more pensive and reflective types, who discover—and invent—adventures in quiet library alcoves, down back alleys, on barstools, in front of the fire, in their interior life; maybe with a donkey somewhere, going slow, perhaps even in a field watching your tail swish about, Gribouille. Between each swish, in the blurry zone between what is real and what is imagined, we find true adventure, what Mac Orlan called *passive adventuring*.

Perhaps we're really *passive* adventurers, Gribouille,

like Mac Orlan said, solitary explorers, in narrower contact with the past, wandering a lot and daydreaming often. In our adventures, we find only trees to sit under, lentils to munch, paths to wander down, loose horses to steer around, and time to find ourselves, to discover what we're really made of. Maps and compasses aren't necessary. Voyages are more commonplace, more everyday; less risky for sure, yet more sustainable, and perhaps, just perhaps, more compelling: they're as dangerous as we want them to be. But beware, my friend: there's nothing to conquer here, nobody to beat—except yourself, of course.

That night, after visiting the museum, I followed the advice of its curator, Madame Baron, and went to eat at Le Plat d'Étain. Monsieur Legrand, *le patron,* is a portly, jovial man with a small white moustache who greets diners at the door in a bow tie. The "pewter plate" itself rests on the wall in the modest *salle à manger,* which, as per custom in France, is hushed and well illuminated. The Beef Bourguignon tasted all the better knowing I'd been sitting in Mac Orlan's old pew. "Oh yes, he was a regular," Monsieur Legrand told me enthusiastically. "He'd sit over there with his friends, wearing a tam-o'-shanter, puffing on his pipe and telling stories." Monsieur Legrand was happy knowing somebody was still interested in the late Monsieur Mac Orlan and in Frédé and Lolo, and in all those reprobates whose memory is consecrated everywhere around here. I was happy that Monsieur Legrand was happy.

Once outside, in the cold half-light of a single feeble streetlamp, I was struck with what Mac Orlan said in another one of his hundred-odd books: "It's the finest quality of the French that they can render agreeable a block of houses, a few farms, two or three lamplights, and a sad café where you can die of boredom playing dominoes. It isn't so much that, on this vast earth, the French are nicer than anybody else, but more that they know how to bring a bit of pleasantry to their little existence."

✤

I've seen a good number of those sad cafés myself, usually each morning, just as we get set to start out. I try to attach Gribouille somewhere and go in for a quick coffee that's often not that quick, given that owners have no real reason to be quick. I order, come back out again, look for a spot to sit outside so I can keep on eye on my companion. Most often there'll be someone inside, an old faithful, no matter what hour, sitting alone, staring into space, into the dimness, hand around a glass of *eau de vie*. The atmosphere is typically melancholic, musty, and moldy: the three "Ms" of the French village café. Some bars double up as tiny newsagents selling dailies, magazines, and cigarettes; occasionally they'll have bread, be *dépôts de pain*, or act as surrogate grocers' stores. At first, these little places struck me as dead and depressing, and I'd shiver upon entering; yet, gradually, I came to understand them, began to feel the pleasantry of this little existence, see their merit in a world flooded with false light. They're places where you can drift off into a slumber, invent adventures in your head, and perhaps play dominoes with a donkey.

What a contrast with my New York days. I never found anywhere public in Manhattan where I could sit in melancholic half-light, alone, quietly poring over my morning coffee, my black liquid peace, drinking it out of a real cup, and with a saucer, readying myself to face life for another earth day. Back then, instead, I lapped up the nonstop talking and action, the lines and frenzy, the busyness and the paper cups, even normalized it all; and, after a while, searched it out. I thought it exciting and stimulating, energizing and liberating, to be sitting among masses of bodies in relative anonymity, without anybody ever noticing me.

Gribouille isn't far away. He's attached to Céaux d'Allegre's cenotaph's railings, at the village crossroads. There's a patch of grass to nibble on. He's content enough for a while. I can see him from where I'm sitting, from a café terrace, really a couple of wooden tables under a faded awning advertising Fanta. The café is empty inside, only the patron there washing glasses; his mongrel dozes under a barstool. It's late afternoon and cloudy overhead, a bit dull, a strange change in the weather, unseasonably cold. Not a lot happening around here. Saturday afternoon. At least, I think it's Saturday afternoon. A few teenage kids pass by on bikes. I hear them mutter something about the donkey and laugh, but don't catch exactly what was said.

I'm drinking a big cup of coffee, strong, without cream or sugar, thinking about what happens when all the effervescence disappears, when all the dynamism you once had in your life is henceforth put into slow motion. And when the crowds have gone, too. If I sit alone like this, in the quietness, others don't distract me; I can't go elsewhere with *them,* can't tap into their cell-phone conversations, or loud interactions with one another, even if I wanted to; now I no longer *find* distractions like that. I'm simply here and must confront myself in that hereness. It's surprising how difficult I found this. Initially, I felt a void, a sort of withdrawal symptom; I suppose I was going cold turkey because I *missed* the distraction. Moreover, I stood out like a sore thumb, sitting alone with my petit coffee, speaking with a strange accent, not knowing anybody. That made me self-conscious. Not always a good thing! And the *there* I once had, had been taken away. I felt an eerie lack of content, a lack of thereness to my hereness. I was nowhere, am nowhere. And yet, soon, little by little, interesting things began to happen to me; voids steadily got filled in and an unassuming richness crept up on me, a lucid presentness.

Being noticed isn't so bad anyway. Losing that anonymous cover forces you out into the open. So who is that guy over there with the donkey? Good question: ask it to yourself sometime! In the tranquility, I also began to recognize how that whirl of life, that dazzling dynamism I sought out, is a kind of adult escapism, a sort of cheap adventuring, with little sustainable behind it. And it doesn't take much imagination to participate. It's like living life staring at shop-window mannequins: changing fashions, changing clothes, but only in two dimensions. If you catch a sudden glance of yourself in that shop window, you might glimpse another mannequin, on the move, walking down the sidewalk, fast.

Around here, there are few window displays, and

absolutely no surface gloss, whizz, or razzmatazz. The band strikes up only a few times a year at fêtes and on July 14, on Bastille Day, and it's invariably out of tune. And those speeches given by village mayors go on and on! But if you sit here long enough, and if you just about stay awake, you'll feel a texturing that's thicker, a culture and tradition that's discretely enduring, that's somehow baked into a baguette, churned into a morsel of cheese, and brewed into a little cup of coffee drunk in a sad café corner. It's a humble charm that enters through the back door, unannounced. A passive adventurer's muse . . .

30

ALLEZ-HOP! WE'RE OFF going south, headed toward lower, gentler land, toward the Allier Gorge. For the first time I feel that I know where to go, have a clear plan ahead, about where we're destined to end up. I'll tell you about it soon, a bit later on. Beforehand, we need to get nearer to the windmills, nearer toward Ally. *Les éoliennes*, locals call them, giant windmills, after the Greek wind god Aeolus, modern electricity-producing monsters that would terrify Don Quixote, rows of them, running along the horizon. "See those over yonder, with vast arms some of which are two leagues long." Once we see them, we'll know we're arriving, we'll know good fortune is guiding our affairs; we'll know they're really giants.

We'll need to leave the Livradois Forest soon and wend our way toward the west, toward Jax, following the setting sun. There'll be some meandering trails to navigate, as well as narrow stretches of asphalt, spiraling downward, trees either side. Out of the forest, the landscape will open up before us. We'll see for miles, more than a 180-degree panorama, a gigantic open-air amphitheater, with great views of rolling hills, of high-peaked volcanoes that last erupted eight thousand years ago, of Puy du Sancy and Puy-de-Dôme, trailing off all the way to Clermont-Ferrand. The eye has to adjust to an immense repertoire of green.

The path is dusty and full of loose red boulders. I sense that Gribouille isn't moving quite right; he's stopping frequently, just standing there, not wanting to advance. This is strange, because it's easy going. We're edging downhill gently. Let's get that packsaddle off and check those feet, see if there's a problem somewhere. I've got this small cloth bag of tricks, with a few currycombs, a little jar of white herbal ointment, a kind of paste—for putting on a wound near Gribouille's left eye, where flies tend to gather; a ball of string; and a couple of hoof picks. I tap just below his knee, along the cannon bone, on one back leg. He obliges and lifts up his foot. Nothing much there, only a gathering of mud; I clean it out, working from heel to toe, really scraping. Nothing, either, trapped in the foot of his other hind leg. But in the front left there are big, big pebbles lodged in the frog, stuck hard; you need to be firm getting rid of them, and reasonably quick because Gribouille is balancing himself. That's it: I think I've found the cause of his unwillingness to move.

❦

I wipe my hands on my shorts, which are now getting filthy; I'm looking increasingly rough, like a vagrant, with heavy facial growth and in serious need of a wash and change of clothes. If I keep this up, in a while we'll look like Frédé and Lolo, an *Auvergnat* Robinson Crusoe strolling with Man Friday, waving vainly at passing ships. People will start veering off soon, begin to avoid us as I approach, as we clip-clop into town. I'm yearning to sleep in my own bed. Yet onward we go. Donkeys' hooves are fascinating things when you think about them, when you inspect them carefully. Different from horses: littler, daintier, steeper, like baby feet. But those baby feet are tougher and more elastic than any horse's. For that reason, donkeys essentially walk barefoot in the park: they don't normally need to be shod, don't normally wear blacksmith-made shoes. What they're walking on is all natural, all skin and bone and organic tissue, like horn, tiny spiral horn tubules, or like human toenails, which get long unless they're cut regularly.

Foot hygiene is vital for a donkey, just as athlete's foot and ingrown toenails aren't much fun for us. It's one reason why donkeys aren't keen on very hard surfaces or paths with lots of rough, tough stones. It's also why foot problems are pretty common. To ensure good hoof growth, blood circulation and regular expansion are necessary. This means keeping mobile, doing adequate amounts of walking. Experts say that to maintain natural hoof growth, donkeys should cover around ten miles a day on reasonably firm surfaces. They say that donkey hooves have "naturally" adapted to movement, to keeping busy. Sedentary donkeys, just like sedentary humans, aren't usually the healthiest.

Wild donkeys, those who forage for food and water day in, day out and cover a lot of ground, likely won't ever need their feet trimmed. They'll probably develop other problems anyway. If a farrier doesn't trim a domesticated donkey's feet every ten weeks or so, they'll keep growing and growing. He'll skillfully cut up the frog, clean everything out—soil and mud and stones—and *balance* the hoof. This is like balancing the wheels of a car to ensure smooth flow and equal wear and tear of the tires. Balancing a donkey's hooves will center the animal's weight distribution, verify the symmetry of its gait, and ensure proper shock absorption.

You can always tell a mistreated donkey by the state of its feet. Clean and healthy donkey feet mean happy little tap-dancing feet, and a happy donkey, even if they never show it. I remember my mother always said that you could judge a man by the condition of his shoes. God knows what she'd say now if she saw these boots of mine, beat up and smelly, ragged and worn, as if I've secretly slipped on the pair of peasant boots that Van Gogh painted. A person without means, of dubious character? Somebody whom they'd never let their daughter marry?

❧

There's an unforgettable image of a donkey's hooves in *Au Hasard Balthazar*, a frankly stunning scene. It's impossible to leave that movie behind. Somehow Balthazar has become the property of a semivagrant drunk, Arnold, a man who's hauntingly gaunt, with a black beard. Arnold lives in a wooden shack in the middle of the woods and dresses like a World War One army vet, in a disheveled trench coat. Sometimes it seems he's a bit shell-shocked. It's not clear exactly how, but one day Arnold's luck changes: he inherits a fortune, and at Gérard's party, the night of the firecrackers, Arnold goes for it. Urged on by Gérard, he knocks back whiskey after whiskey. Strangely, rather than celebrate, Arnold gets sadder and sadder as the night wears on; he drinks to offset his misfortune, perhaps the misfortune of his inheritance, of now being rich. The party becomes ever more raucous and Arnold ever more drunk, ever more bent on self-destruction. In the early hours, Gérard and his friends bid Arnold good-night and help him mount Balthazar, bareback, maybe knowing what lies ahead. Arnold staggers aboard. Balthazar walks off into the deathly nighttime air.

Out of town, along the road, in the pitch-black silence, Arnold stops his donkey. He looks up at an electricity pylon; the camera freezes up there for a moment. Then Arnold begins his final, guilt-ridden farewells: good riddance to the world, he says, and to the folly of its cruel ways, including his own. But his real valediction is to Balthazar, who listens, all ears: "Farewell, my loyal friend, condemned to stay here and watch the same imbeciles go by!" Then Arnold topples, throws himself off purposefully, nose-diving from Balthazar. Suddenly, the action switches into slow motion, prolonging and amplifying the drama of the Fall. Arnold's head crashes on the asphalt, a modern road surface much traveled along by humans. There's a close-up, an amazingly long close-up, of Arnold's bashed-in head next to Balthazar's lower legs and hooves. The hooves jar the viewer as anachronistic, as the bearer of some primordial truth. They're absolutely motionless. We never see Balthazar's face but can imagine his unfathomable gaze staring out into the deep, dark distance. Never have a donkey's hooves assumed such a gravity of meaning, revealed so much about human destiny.

31

I CAN PRACTICALLY grip my hands around a donkey's legs, around its cannon bones and fetlocks and pastern joints. They're that skinny. A donkey's back is incredibly strong, incredibly solid—like a rock, we know; but it's those little legs and hooves that prop up the back, that take the strain and walk with such surety. The first time I saw donkeys really taking up the strain, Gribouille, was in Morocco. It left a big impression on me, a really big impression. I was in Marrakech, sat in gentle November sunshine, on a wooden bench not far from the Souk, the old Medina, watching the chaos of the city, a chaos I could have lived without, wished I wasn't around. I had no interest in Moroccan carpets or in trinkety lamps, or in leather bags and caftan coats; in fact, I'd no interest in anything peddled before me, shoved in my face at the bazaar. Indeed, I wasn't really sure why I'd come, why I was sat there, why I was wandering in the crowds.

Yet I was interested in donkeys. It was an interest I never knew I had. I was discovering something new, something hitherto buried in myself; I was being touched by something there and then. It's taken me a while to work it out, this revelatory moment. They were everywhere; I'd never seen so many donkeys, right in the heart of the city, right at the core of that city's economic life, despite the Mercedes whizzing by, despite the glitzy banks and gaping tourists. Yes, Marrakech's economy, both its formal and informal sort, was still a cart-and-donkey affair, still had donkeys transporting wood and wares, car engines and vegetables. It's hard to describe, but, sitting on this bench like an alien from another galaxy, I felt completely *at two* from what was happening around me, utterly cut off from the tourists and hustlers, from an energy everybody told me was infectious, told me I ought to like.

The only connection I had in Morocco was with those donkeys. I was communing with them. They moved me, stirred something inside me: their composure, their tranquility, their strength, it was amazing, admirable. Human beings were lightweights, I kept thinking, compared to donkeys, weaker, less profound. Noise levels around town were deafening; the air was full of smog and dirt and grime and tobacco. And yet donkeys stood there unconcerned, heads bowed, a little sad, above it all, beyond it all. Their facial expressions remained unflappably calm, peaceful in themselves, almost invincible. I wanted to walk around town and pat every one, embrace them, follow Samuel Taylor Coleridge and proclaim my loyalty, my undying affinity: "I love the languid patience of thy face: / And oft with gentle hand I give thee bread, / And clap thy ragged coat, and pat thy head . . . I hail thee *Brother!*" I saw many donkeys whose rumps were hairless and bloody, whose owners whacked them often, with a cudgel, in the exact same place. Their wounds were raw and open and covered with flies. Each time I raised my hand to pat their heads, many of the donkeys flinched away, winced and awaited a blow. They were that unaccustomed to affection. Nobody ever stroked them. I had to coax them into accepting my caresses.

Moroccan donkeys had also made a lasting impression on a consumptive George Orwell, who'd wintered in Marrakech in 1939 to improve his ailing health. This was four years before he'd begin writing *Animal Farm* (penned between November 1943 and February 1944), and it may have been there, in Marrakech, where Orwell first imagined Old Benjamin, first dreamed up his great philosopher donkey, the nemesis of autocracy: "I had not been five minutes on Moroccan soil before I noticed the overloading of the donkeys and was infuriated by it. There is no question that the donkeys are damnably treated. The

Moroccan donkey is hardly bigger than a Saint Bernard dog; it carries a load which in the British army would be considered too much for a fifteen-hands mule, and very often its packsaddle is not taken off its back for weeks together. But what is peculiarly pitiful is that it is the most willing creature on earth, it follows its master like a dog and does not need either bridle or halter. After a dozen years of devoted work it suddenly drops dead, whereupon its master tips it into the ditch and the village dogs have torn its guts out before it is cold."

African popular legend claims that every human has an animal equivalent, an animal other, a double. Had I found mine in North Africa, in Morocco, my Saint Bernard dog, sitting on that bench, on the sunny side of the street? It was the first time I'd been warm in days. My mind wandered in the autumnal glow. I began to conceive a plan for a book, sketched out loosely in draft, a book about donkeys, about their human double, a different book from what I'd written before, more personal, more graphic, more honest somehow. The warmth was nice because I'd been frozen most of the time in the mountains, up in the Atlas Mountains, near Ouirgane, forty miles from Marrakech. I'd been there several days earlier, at an inn called Le Sanglier qui Fume—"The Wild Boar who Smokes"—a former French Foreign Legion outpost, later a haunt for wild-boar hunters, now a frayed staging post for trekkers and tourists. Snow-capped peaks with orange-soil foothills surround this Smoking Wild Boar. The sky was turquoise, I remember that, utterly cloudless.

I remember following a donkey laden with a huge

pile of firewood, watching him in action, head bowed, the epitome of concentration. There was a minimountain stacked on his back, on the back of a donkey half your size, Gribouille. He negotiated a path no more than two feet wide, really a ridge in the earth, perched over a death-defying incline. He measured every step, precisely placed each hoof. His skinny legs wilted from the strain. But he was moving and enduring. There were a lot of donkeys out carrying firewood, pale-colored, bone-dry branches, stacked up. Alas, few seemed to be carrying firewood to the Smoking Wild Boar. There was no heating in my room other than a big, ornate open fire. It looked like a terra-cotta kiln, the sort of place where you'd bake bread. At first blush, everything here seemed grand: regal red sofas, ele-gant dark-wood coffee tables, lush curtains, soft bed linen. But the terra-cotta fireplace was pointless without wood; and apparently there wasn't much wood to be had at the Smoking Wild Boar, save a couple of measly morsels. And once they started to burn, the room was overcome with clouds of swirling white smoke. There was little heat gen-erated. Frostbite and bronchitis awaited me. I couldn't get warm. I couldn't stop coughing. I hoped I was going to make it till morning.

Earlier that day, I'd been following Omar, my guide, who zipped along despite a serious limp. For a few hours, from late morning till about three in the afternoon, in the open air, it was gloriously balmy. I was happy to follow Omar, to zip along with him, following a sinking sun. A car had hit Omar a while back, and the leg wound still pained him. He raised the bottom of his pants and showed me a large, half-open gash; it looked as if there was a metal plate inside. He squeezed it and a red pus gushed out. Coming toward us were more donkeys, carrying wood, and, after them, others carrying wheat. Up and down the mountain they'd go, each and every day, all the time, a big-eared relay system, transporting goods as well as their masters, some of whom rode sidesaddle.

An hour beyond the Smoking Wild Boar we encountered isolated Berber villages; a few had primitive generators for electricity, with makeshift wires dangling overhead; nobody had heating. Villagers dry their clothes on south-facing hillsides. As I approached, I could see little blobs of coloring on rock faces: reds and yellows, oranges and blues. For a while, we followed the same track as two Berber kids, two beautiful little girls, ascending the mountain, going home after school, wrapped up in head scarves. Occasionally they'd look back, sneak a glance at me, and snigger. Outside their house the kids shyly asked, in broken French, if I had *un stylo* to give them, a pen. I handed them one of my many blue felt-tipped Paper Mates.

Their mother invited Omar and me into a simple stone house. We sat cross-legged on a mat in a square room bereft of furniture. A tray was brought to us with an ornate pot and little cups and saucers, and we drank very sweet mint tea. Then an old woman, the kids' grandmother, cooked us a delicious omelet with home-baked bread. Tied up outside were the family's two donkeys, their lifeline, a pair of silver-grays with glowing white legs, magic donkeys. I'd seen them earlier tilling a fallow field next to olive groves, tilling the hard way, through brute strength, dragging a wooden plow straight out of preindustrialized England. Donkeys act as the modern machinery farmers don't have and will never get. In awe, I patted them both when I left. They were standing there, looking soft and childlike again, no longer indomitable beasts of burden. I looked at those skinny white legs, at those little dainty hooves, eight of them in a row, eight tap-dancing miracles, in the sunny light of day.

And so, Gribouille, on that bench in Marrakech, drifting in its daily donkey life, thinking about the cold, about the Smoking Wild Boar, about its room full of smoke, I think I really did experience a strange epiphany. It helped bring us together. I'm not sure how, precisely, but it did; it led me here with you. I'd glimpsed your working cousins in action. Afterward, I'd wanted to learn more, wanted more detailed instruction. So I found a way to go to Egypt, Gribouille, the cradle of the donkey.

32

THE GIZA COUNTRYSIDE was fascinating, exotically surreal. The great pyramids of Cheops, Chefren, and Menkaure flashed by, out in the distance, in among palm trees and the green, surprisingly green, flat arable land, and the desert with its big rolling dunes, enchanting folds of corrugated gold, which seemed less real in reality. All around, too, were buildings, low-rise apartment buildings, that seemed unfinished, that had upper floors gaping. It looked like people had run out of time, or money, to complete them, to cap them off, to put windows in, to seal in the walls. And you should've seen those giant, bony buffalo grazing under the date trees, in their makeshift pens, alongside sheep and goats. Egyptians eat buffalo meat, slaughter males for it, and drink the milk of females, or make butter out of it. Buffalos tower over the skinny little donkeys.

Some people think camels were Egypt's traditional beast of burden. But camels weren't introduced until around 525 B.C., when the Persians took control of the country, whereas bones from the earliest known donkey were found in a Maadi cemetery, and the Maadis settled near Cairo in predynastic times, around 4,000–3,500 B.C., thousands of years before the arrival of camels and the Persians. Later on, in Dynastic Egypt, from 3,000 B.C. onward, *the* most important load-bearers were donkeys: a continuous procession of donkeys, carrying water and wheat grain, sustained ancient Egyptian civilization, the civilization that gave us the pyramids. In long-distance trading across the arid Egyptian deserts, donkeys were indispensable: packs trekked from the Nile Valley down Wadi Hammamat and onward to the Red Sea to trade with Arabia. In the second millennium B.C., donkeys eventually made it to Europe, accompanying the introduction of viticulture, carrying grapes on their backs. In fact it was the Greeks who brought both the vine and donkeys to the northern Mediterranean coast, to Italy, Spain, and southern

France. The Romans deployed donkeys to build the roads that donkeys themselves trekked along, continuing their dispersal into Europe while they helped the Romans disperse an Empire.

For the ancient Egyptians, donkeys plowed the desert land and helped brew beer, transporting the barley in the fermenting process—even lugging around assorted kings and queens, like Queen Hetepheres: wooden carrying-chairs, a sort of early saddle, were adapted and strapped to the back of donkeys, examples of which you can now find in Boston's Museum of Fine Arts. And although Egyptians brutalized their little donkeys, they also thought donkeys possessed sacred gifts: donkey milk was considered a luxury drink, as well as the secret to eternal youth. Cleopatra, who reigned between 51 and 30 B.C., kept a stable of three hundred donkeys; each day she bathed in donkey milk, believing it the key to skin health and a recipe in age prevention. She was right: donkey milk is full of fatty acids and vitamins A, E, and F, and it has natural dermatological qualities and rejuvenescent powers, effective for dry, wrinkled skin.

I got out beyond Cairo and was finally free of its foul air and mad traffic. In the back of a car tooting its horn at passing trucks, we weaved in and out of hundreds and hundreds of donkeys pulling cartloads of fruit and vegetables, sacks of wheat and raw manure, shifting assorted bric-a-brac of poor everyday life in the Egyptian countryside. Nothing here would function without donkeys: without their weight-bearing little legs and hooves, without their rock-solid backs, there'd simply be no Egyptian rural daily life, no merchant comings-and-goings to the market, no farmers plowing their fields, no crop harvesting, no transportation of wares. Sometimes you see them galloping with a heavy cart piled high with salad greens, really running along, building up momentum. The enormous weight motions itself, is a lighter load to drag once it moves: smart work for a slow donkey. Other times you glimpse the special pitter-patter of their cadence, little legs going rapidly back and forth, carrying their masters, and moving mountains almost as big as the nearby pyramids.

Those pyramids were nicer from a distance. I'd been there the day before, partaken in the tourist spectacle. I wasn't sure if I was glimpsing the real thing or had suddenly beamed down in Las Vegas. Was it a nightmare or a dream? Was there a difference? Who could decipher what was genuine from what was fake? It all felt very phony, very *de*-naturalized, squalid somehow, humiliating. The coaches arrived, the people flocked, the hawkers touted their plastic pyramids, their little cheap sphinxes; everybody wanted your money, wanted to take your picture. Cigarette butts littered sacred desert earth. Tour guides appeared as New Age healers whose repertoire was Cockney rhyming slang. Should I laugh or cry? How had an ancient culture become so tacky and pathetic?

But that was yesterday. Now it was Monday morning, another desert Monday, in Aoseem. I'd arrived under palm trees drooping with dates, in a disheveled and dusty village square, surrounded by mounds of flotsam and jetsam, by plastic bags and corn plant stalks. There were no real roads in the village, just rough, uneven dirt tracks, and people living in those unfinished concrete buildings. Dogs scavenged scraps. Murky streams that may have been tributaries of the Nile flowed nearby. At the marketplace were tables piled high with fresh fruit and cafés where men sat outside, smoking and drinking tea. The dusty square was full of older men and young boys, and donkeys, lots and lots of donkeys; and braying, loud soulful braying, donkey lingua franca, the language every donkey understands.

Today was the outdoor clinic of the Society for the Protection and Welfare of Donkeys and Mules in Egypt (SPWDME). Each week a fully equipped mobile unit visits eleven villages around Giza and Kalubia, offering free treatment for damaged, abused, and overworked donkeys. SPWDME has its work cut out. There were perhaps seventy or so downtrodden donkeys that morning, standing a little dejectedly, a little bludgeoned by life, battered and battle-worn, heads held low despite the fine autumn sunshine, waiting for vet Dr. Mohsen Hassan to look them over, to offer his diagnosis, and to administer treatment. He's one of the calmest and most patient young men I'd seen for a long while, in his early thirties, donned in the blue T-shirt and baseball cap of the clinic's main donor: the Sidmouth Donkey Sanctuary.

The old farmers and merchants, the tanned and sometimes toothless veterans I saw before me, dressed in long cotton robes and beat-up sandals, are totally reliant on donkeys for their livelihood. Sometimes a lone woman stepped forth with a donkey, perhaps a farmer's wife, perhaps a widow. Everybody makes their animals work hard, and bringing injured or sick donkeys to a clinic means loss of a morning's income, serious stuff for a poor farmer. That's why working donkeys don't get treated as often as they should. That's perhaps why wives often show up.

Mohsen reckoned much maltreatment is based on ignorance rather than cruelty. These people, he said, don't understand that donkeys feel pain. Local kids were sometimes the worst donkey-bashers: they treat donkeys like they treat their bikes, if they have bikes: like machines, like they're nonsensuous, nonfeeling things, not living creatures. In fact, Mohsen said, local kids treat donkeys worse than bikes, whacking them with wooden batons, pushing and kicking them, sometimes just for fun, just for hell of it. What a difference from their western counterparts; a cultural difference, perhaps, a difference in perception: a work tool compared to a fluffy curiosity? It's one reason why Mohsen begins each mobile clinic with a lecture on donkey welfare. It's equally why the SPWDME organizes regular school visits to raise kids' awareness about *respect*—respect for a donkey.

People were standing in front of a chart, hung on a tree, listening to Mohsen's advice. Even the donkeys seemed interested—or at least curious. In among the small crowd, I had my arm around the head of one little gray whose ears were pricked up attentively; I felt the warmth of a donkey who walked with an appalling hobble and who had string sewn into the flesh of one thigh. Mohsen talked around the chart's colorful, clear images, discoursing on how to evenly load a cart, how to sit correctly on a donkey, how to notice lameness, how to prevent saddle wounds, how to detect signs of illness and injury, how to refresh a donkey in summer heat, how to tie a harness, etc., etc. Because of its preventive edge, this teach-in session is a vital component of the clinic; many donkey problems, Mohsen lamented to me afterward, could be avoided with sensible handling practice and informed care. He was always disappointed when owners showed up late and missed his lecture.

It was first come, first served at the clinic, except I noticed how women got preferential treatment, were often seen straightaway. When owners arrived, they signed the logbook; illiterate ones used thumbprints. A clinic lasts until every donkey is treated; sometimes this goes on well into midafternoon, and it's nonstop drama. At the very first clinic, back in 2002, Mohsen told me he treated 214 donkeys. It turned out that the donkey I hugged a moment ago has a lot of problems. I was hunched over his hoof after Mohsen lifted it up and began pointing stuff out. There was a huge abscess hidden by dirt and grime. This poor donkey was effectively lame and needed to stop working; and his hooves needed trimming. His plight was salvageable. Mohsen asked the owner if he had another donkey he could use as a replacement. Yes, he has another donkey. This one here, Mohsen said, needs resting for at least two weeks. "No work, okay, d'you understand?" The old farmer nodded in agreement.

Then the vet in the blue baseball cap cleaned out the abscess with a special pick. One of his two assistants expertly restrained the poor abscessed beast, prevented him from naturally fleeing the pain he was feeling in his hoof. The assistant put his arms gently around the whole of his head. He showed the owner how to be firm yet kind toward his donkey. Owners had a habit of gripping a donkey's ears, twisting them around and around as if you were wringing out a damp cloth. The assistant tut-tutted this kind of restraining behavior. Mohsen swilled out the abscess with iodine, then applied a thick tarlike paste, and I saw the whites of the helpless donkey's eyes, whites of eyes that revealed private pain, heartbreaking eyes, eyes of profaned innocence. I was terribly moved and felt deep pity. I'd never seen the whites of a donkey's eyes before.

Then a gauze compress was fitted and a giant bandage wrapped around the injured hoof. And the string sewn into the flesh, at the top of the same leg, string the owner's neighbor had said would help treat the lameness, that had gone septic; it needed careful removal, and the fluid from the swelling needed draining. Mohsen gave the donkey a tetanus vaccination and an anti-inflammatory shot. He'd seen the like before, he said, seen such hocus-pocus medicine, and pointed to other lame donkeys who had been purposefully cut with knives, and whose wounds eventually go bad; owners really believe cutting is curative, that blood-letting helps, that threading cords under the skin, inside the flesh, is medicinal.

"What happened there?" I enquired, pointing and wincing at a skinny gray with two hollow stumps masquerading as ears. Mohsen fired off something in Arabic. The owner responded, saying his donkey once strayed into another farmer's field and started eating that farmer's corn. The farmer came storming over, mad as hell, a little crazy; and, as punishment, brandishing his machete, sliced off part of the donkey's ears. The donkey bolted away, howling with pain, with blood spilling everywhere ...

All that happened a few years back, and now the wounds have healed. The stumps looked strange, though, another pitiful, heartbreaking sight. Today, this poor half-eared donkey was losing weight. "Worms," Mohsen told me, "he's got worms. Very common around here." The vet injected the donkey with something, then squirted liquid into his mouth with a plastic syringe, and handed the owner a little bag of white powder to administer each day. The farmer wandered off with his ragged, skinny donkey with two stub ears. I watched them both disappear, wondering whether these people ever followed Mohsen's advice; I wondered whether they could really *afford* to follow Mohsen's advice.

❧

Many farmers in poorer parts of the world will tell you that a donkey isn't only as strong as an ox; in a lot of instances it's a good deal stronger—certainly pound for pound. They'll point out to you that it's possible to plow the land with a single donkey, that donkeys are easier to train than oxen, that they're hardier, more able to tolerate drought conditions, less susceptible to disease in dry seasons; and that donkeys are multipurpose: they can plow, carry water and firewood, grind the mill, transport maize, and be ridden. And they're cheaper to maintain than an ox.

Meanwhile, their placid, gentler nature means women can more easily handle them. Indeed, the "lowly" status of donkeys often has them designated a woman's beast. In developing countries, women might control donkeys even if they can't ever sell one without their husband's permission. These gender differences in donkey use have a few beneficial outcomes, since they relieve women of much of the burden of everyday chores, of the massive water jugs they'd otherwise have to haul for miles and miles across barren mountainous countryside, like they do in Ethiopia. Donkeys also help women prosper in small farm holdings, like in western Zambia, where cattle-raising is seen as man's work. In Kenya, a donkey water bearer apparently saves Maasai women up to twenty-five hours per week in labor time, freeing them up for other activities at home and in the community.

Average life expectancy for a donkey in Ethiopia is around nine years; in Egypt it's eleven years; in Kenya and Mexico and China it's about fourteen years; for a domesticated European and North American donkey, for you and your friends, it's nearer thirty-five years, occasionally forty; very occasionally, if you're lucky, you might top fifty. (At the Sidmouth Donkey Sanctuary, I remember seeing a blind, gray old-timer who was approaching sixty years old!) In South Africa, donkey longevity is feted in local folklore: if a donkey shows up at a wedding, it's said that the couple's grandchildren will see it.

In poor developing countries, for the bulk of their populations, donkey power is more ubiquitous, and more vital, than the internal combustion engine. So if a donkey gets sick or can't work, it's the end of the road; people are tipped over the edge, go down with their donkeys. Thus a donkey is a family lifeline, a provider as well as a car. Donkeys do it without respite, and invariably without refreshment. You eat lush grass, Gribouille, have a lovely shining coat, and to a certain degree so do I; we're both lucky. But other donkeys elsewhere, in developing countries, in sub-Saharan Africa, are skinny and eat scraps of rubbish they find by the roadside, have poor, ragged, mangy coats, just like their master's. Global donkey inequities mimic the human world's inequities.

⁂

Other overworked donkeys appeared, and Mohsen's casualty line lengthened. As healthy donkeys passed by, dragging laden carts, they brayed vigorously, said hi to old friends, empathized with damaged brethren. Perhaps they brayed because they might be next. Mohsen handled every donkey professionally, lovingly, administering his healing hand with tender care rather than complacent haste. He was back and forth to the medicine chest that was laid out on the open rear door of a white pickup truck. The commonest problem, he said, was poorly fitted harnesses, as well as saddles bearing too-heavy loads. If you peer beneath the rug that's under a donkey's saddle, you can see how a heavy weight creates really bad skin irritation and scuffing. Usually the skin is worn away and an open wound is apparent.

To cleanse these wounds, Mohsen trimmed the hair with surgical scissors and applied antiseptic lotion. One white donkey he was working on looked like he'd seen action on the frontline of a war zone. *Le pauvre!* He had massive sores all over his body; hair and flesh had literally been rubbed away, stripped off, revealing bleeding, raw gashes. And the owner had plastered these open wounds with manure, thinking it would cure them. The pain from the wounds, to say nothing about the manure, must have been excruciating. Yet for once these wounds were self-inflicted. For the real source of the problem was *colic*: acute abdominal pains and gastrointestinal difficulties. The donkey wasn't passing feces, Mohsen said. And in trying to relieve the agony of his stomach pains, he rolled over violently, dragged himself through hard, dusty desert ground, exacerbating his torment by creating these dreadful sores. Soon the animal was covered with iodine and his white coat had suddenly turned dark orange; Mohsen injected him with something and again squirted a colorless liquid into his mouth. It was incredible how tranquil this battered beast was. It was as if he knew he needed curing, that curing the colic would stop him rolling, would help heal those wounds.

"We need to replace that harness," Mohsen said, inspecting the next wounded soldier. Friction sores were frequent because owners intentionally used chains around their donkey's muzzle. When they wanted to break their donkey, they pulled on the lead rope attached to his harness. The chain dug into the donkey's flesh, letting him know he needed to stop. That hurt. But it was the hurting that restrained the donkey from doing anything else but stop. Mohsen spends a lot of time treating infected wounds caused by these chains. To avoid such chafing, SPWDME gives out free donkey-friendly *cotton* harnesses. I was surprised that Mohsen had to show many farmers how to retie a donkey's harness.

Nearby, a second assistant applied antibiotic drops to a donkey's eyes; owners rarely, if ever, cleaned their donkeys' eyes. This donkey had a parasitic infection caused by flies, and it was spreading down his face. Unwashed eyes are prone to infection: flies actually lay eggs in and around a donkey's eyes and, if unchecked, their larvae spread. There was a thin sliver of a wound, a blood-red gash stemming from one eye that looked bothersome. You've got to cleanse those eyes, treat the wound, and somehow keep flies at bay. Here the "fly mask" came into its own, a light mesh bonnet, with elasticated straps, that fits snugly over an infected donkey's face. It was an endearing sight, seeing a donkey in a fly mask. It seemed to emphasize the childlike vulnerability of creatures who were unable, even unwilling, to kill a fly, to swat a perennial pest.

❦

"Around Cairo, the price of donkeys has gone up a lot in past years," Mohsen said, talking to me in the back of a car returning to SPWDME's Giza office in Faisal. We were crawling along, bumper to bumper, going nowhere terribly fast. "There are fewer breeders breeding donkeys these days," Mohsen continued. "That means the few donkeys they do breed sell at very high prices. It's a big expense for farmers in the Giza area. Renewing their donkey, or else buying another, becomes very difficult now. So the donkeys they have are even more precious, and even more overworked."

Out of the car window I watched daily life roll by, gaping at some of the sixteen million people who populate metropolitan Cairo. A few stared back at me. For a fleeting instant our eyes met, sometimes as two slits peeping through a veil: who were these men and women, busying themselves *en masse*? And who was that guy there, their eyes wondered back. Donkeys were pulling carts around town, in the traffic, in air that reeked of car emissions. In alleyways of crowded apartment blocks, you saw little donkeys tied to gateposts, sharing space with neighborhood canines. Then I asked Mohsen whether he enjoyed his job as a donkey vet. "I love my job," he stated, very simply, smiling, without a moment's hesitation. "It makes me happy to heal these animals." He stayed silent for a moment, as if still mulling the question over in his own mind, and added: "Yes, I get happiness from healing."

He isn't the only one: in healing these hurt lifelines for the poor, these battered beasts of burden, he's helping the poor survive, helping them hang on. So poor farmers, too, are happy Mohsen is happy healing, even if they never tell him, even if they never think about it—even if they themselves are often the cause of the problem. It's complex: they treat their donkeys very badly, sometimes with brutal impatience, with ordinary human impatience, yet they value the work their donkeys do. By saving donkeys, Mohsen saves these people. He helps keep everybody going, keeps everybody keeping on; that's effective development, an important job, real dedication. I was a little envious; and, for a second, in the back of the car, I imagined myself in another life as a donkey savior, a life I knew I'd never have. "Happiness from healing," I repeated after Mohsen, mumbling it under my breath. "That's nice . . . real nice."

⚘

Next morning, a little after dawn broke, I was off to the airport in a taxi, a clapped-out old Lada that had already done a few hundred thousand miles. Despite the warmth and sunshine, it had started to rain. The cabbie was having trouble with his windshield wipers. They were pretty useless. The more they tried to clean, the greasier and grimier the windshield became. The net result was solidified smog on a vehicle that likely hadn't been serviced since about 1959. When the sun hit the glass, a dazzling haze was all we could see. Yet the driver refused to slow down and blasted through central Cairo, blindly. Soon we were up above the city, on an expressway that had been hacked through a drab concrete cityscape, looking like the South Bronx. We were literally flying along, yet unable to see ahead. There was a kind of madness to these road habits and I was starting to feel very, very uncomfortable, relishing the idea of being high above it all, in the clouds.

Suddenly, the driver started to decelerate and then came to a complete halt. It was gridlock again; the cabbie just about saw enough in front to stop. It was six o'clock in the morning, on a three-lane highway, and it was already jammed with cars. It was really bucketing it down, too; though the sheer weight of water, piling down, finally began to cleanse the windshield. We could see ahead again. But it wasn't obvious why everybody had stopped. We inched along. I was conscious of time, that I had a flight to catch, that I wanted to be free of this collective insanity.

Before long, I realized it was an accident; I was surprised I'd seen so few. There were all sorts of fruits spread across the tarmac; it looked like a cartload of oranges had toppled over, been hit by a speeding car. As we approached, I saw an old cart sprawled across one lane, lying on its side, an old cart being towed by a donkey; the cars had to swerve around the scene. And then I saw the poor donkey himself, sitting down at the roadside, looking wistful and peaceful with bloodied knees. I couldn't tell whether he was badly hurt or not. I had no idea how it all happened. I can still see him sitting there now, Gribouille, in my mind's eye, sitting tranquilly, amid hundreds of beeping cars, frustrated commuters, fast stationary cars, in pouring rain, on a highway at six o'clock in the morning. Forget about the pyramids. Something has gone wrong here, in this life we lead. The donkey knew it. We all know it.

33

THE PATH IS narrow and rough again, crammed with boulders and with tree roots that have strayed over from the woods. They're fed up with subterranean darkness and push upward toward the light like fearsome hydras.

The ground is uneven, steeply downhill and easy to trip over. We've just passed another morning matins together. Now we're leaving Varennes-Saint-Honorat, with its little bell tower, and making for Jax. There's a ruined barn immediately up ahead.

As we reach the barn, a lone donkey appears; he almost leaps out of a side door. It's as if he knew another donkey was approaching. He's really big, like a horse, with a gray coat that's practically blue; and massive ears, sticking up dramatically. He reminds me of the rare Andalusian donkeys I'd seen in Sidmouth: a pure donkey that reaches sixteen hands in height. Then he starts to bray, one of the loudest brays I'd ever heard, blasting out, rattling the decrepit barn next door. Half of the Haute-Loire will hear it, ringing out like enormous catharsis. Whew!

Moments later he and Gribouille are rubbing noses, sniffing each other, and I'm looking at that barn, which is very gloomy inside and full of dung, a miserable hole. The enclosure where he grazes is insufficiently large, overflowing with nettles and also full of dung. Yet he seems healthy enough: well-trimmed feet and shiny, neatly groomed coat, a striking color. The two donkeys are fascinated by one another. I get the impression our big blue friend doesn't get out much; he's happy to have a bit of company. As I drag Gribouille away, his new pal commences another booming bray.

"Does the wild ass bray when he has grass," asked Job. I feel sad having to move on, having to separate the pairing. Then, as the rattling reverberates across wilderness,

Gribouille responds in kind, with a brief, partial, compassionate bray, a trademark onomatopoeia: *Eeyore! Eeyore! Eeyore!* If you're near a braying donkey, you can really hear the inward and outward phases of breath, the sucking in of air and the exhaling; you can hear the deep, inner source of this mighty guttural utterance. Yet no sooner does it volcanically erupt than Gribouille stops himself; all goes quiet again. And we walk onward, contentedly, as if he needed to get that off his chest.

❦

A braying donkey was considered an ill omen by many ancient Greeks, something they thought heralded misfortune, with demonic proportions. For Aesop, the donkey's bray was the signature tune of stupidity, of a fool's unmistakable trademark. When the donkey dons the lion's skin, says Aesop in "The Ass in the Lion's Skin," and roams the forest frightening other animals, it's the fox who spots the ruse. As the moral goes, clothes may disguise the idiot, but his words will always give him away. Centuries later, however, Dostoevsky cast new light on a donkey's bray. His idiot, Prince Myshkin, heard the bray with different ears, heard it as a kind of awakening, as something curative and wise, as something scaring away demons. Myshkin makes a lot of the braying donkey he hears in Basel's marketplace. This disturbed, and disturbing, young man perplexes his audience when he recounts the experience at Madame Epanchin's house, in the presence of her three daughters. He *amuses* them: he's traveled around Europe and all he wants to talk about is a braying ass!

Tell us about Switzerland, they demand, tell us about your impressions of it. "What affected me most was that everything was *strange*," he says. "I was crushed by the strangeness of it. I was finally aroused from my gloomy state, I remember, one evening on reaching Switzerland, and I was aroused by the bray of an ass in the marketplace. I was immensely struck with the ass, and for some reason extraordinarily pleased with it, and suddenly everything seemed to clear up in my head." "And so, through the ass," he adds, "all Switzerland began to attract me, so that my melancholy passed completely." The girls all laughed.

His interlocutors urge Myshkin to press on with the tale of his Swiss travels: "What did you see abroad besides the ass?" they wonder, impatiently. But soon one daughter begins to recognize his donkey encounter as a kind of parable, an "idiotic" parable with therapeutic powers. "It was clever about the ass," observes Alexandra. "It was interesting what the prince told us of his invalid condition and how one external shock made everything pleasant to him. I've always been interested to know how people go out of their minds and recover again. Especially when it happens all of a sudden."

Dostoevsky's epileptic prince is a naïve man who appears ridiculous in the face of "normal" reality. He's a man whose burning quest is for some supreme human truth. Little wonder he's a profoundly tragic figure, something laughable. Little wonder, too, a donkey's bray should stir his emotions so, should become a sudden shock of awareness for him, a shock of recognition that made everything pleasant again. *Mon semblable, mon frère*. The prince's innocence and naïveté is duly acknowledged through his "other," through the laborious, patient, all-suffering donkey. The prince had heard Schubert's donkey, out in a Swiss marketplace, heard it as a sort of asinine therapy of everyday life. Henceforth, he said, "everything seemed to clear up in my head." And, moreover, everything cleared up "all of a sudden."

❧

The braying I've just heard is rattling my own brain as well. It gets me thinking about an interesting and strange book from the 1970s: *The Primal Scream*, by Arthur Janov. Janov, a California psychologist, seems to redescribe the kind of psychic shock Dostoevsky's Prince Myshkin experienced in the Swiss marketplace: an eerie scream welled up inside a young man lying on the floor of a therapy session, a piercing, deathlike scream that rattled the walls of Janov's office. Afterward, said Janov, after the young man had quieted down, he was flooded with insights: his whole life seemed to have suddenly fallen into place. It was a scream that sounded a lot like a donkey's bray, a lot like Myshkin's own shock of recognition, a psychic transference wherein a donkey's bray becomes a primal scream, a *primal bray*, a scream more intimately human than maybe even we ourselves realize.

The Primal Scream is unmistakable. It has its own quality "of something deep, rattling and involuntary." It happens when defenses are stripped down, when we open ourselves to the naked truth. Anything that builds a stronger defense system, Janov thinks, deepens the neurosis, wells up the tension, encases it. Primal Therapy involves the "dismantling of the causes of tension, defense systems and neurosis. Thus, Primal Theory indicates that the healthiest people are those who are defense-free." We are born nothing but ourselves, Janov writes. "We are not born neurotic or psychotic. We're just born." When defenses go up, they're really defenses against feeling, a fear of feeling, fear of opening oneself up, an inability to breathe freely.

Janov describes the involuntary phases of the Primal Scream: the panting and animalistic sounds; the increasingly rapid and heavy breathing, which at times becomes "locomotive"; then the breathing takes on a life of its own, and broadens and deepens; the stomach is quivering, the chest heaving; the legs are bending and unbending; the head is bobbing from side to side. Suddenly, there's a convulsion, and out of the mouth explodes the powerful scream, the Primal Scream. The uncanny similarity with the stages of the braying donkey, reaching the dramatic climax of a full seven-tonality bray, is curious. Is there a process of transference? Is this what Myshkin was feeling, what he'd experienced in the marketplace? Was he hearing a cry that, if we fully open ourselves to it, rips down our defenses, rattles and reverberates through the very core of our psychic being, leaving us "cleansed" and "pure"? Does Primal Therapy get you to mimic a braying donkey, return you to your childlike purity, to your primordial age of innocence?

The Primal Scream, Janov insists, is a curative process, not merely a temporary release of tension. It seems almost a way to *exorcise* tension. Tension is the central motivant of neurotic behavior, of an inability to switch off, to quieten down, to feel and daydream, to just *be*. Janov puts his finger on our thoroughly modern neurosis, of a person caught up in a whirlpool of distractions, with a mind filled with plans to do, who can't sit still, who thrashes about even in sleep, obsessed with unfinished business, chattering away incessantly by day, crippled by how he or she looks to the world. "Because he is constantly on the move away from his real self," says Janov, "he tends to be flighty—if not physically, then mentally . . . his eyes, like his mind, seem to dart from subject to subject, unable to focus for any length of time."

Primal Therapy—the Primal Bray—works counter-intuitively: you mature as you retrieve your childish needs, you become warm when you feel coldness, become strong through feeling weak, through letting your defenses slip and masks drop; the feeling of the past brings you wholly into the present, and feeling the death of the unreal system brings you back to life. It's the reverse of neurosis, in which you build up a complex defense system, an unreal-ity, when you're afraid but you act brave, feel small but act big to gloss it all over. The Primal Bray, on the other hand, enables people to feel again, to overcome the denial of *honest* feeling. Indeed, the remedy, Janov maintains, is to feel, is to know what feeling is about: to know the *feeling of feeling*.

34

I WONDER WHETHER Janov, in his therapy sessions, ever considered hugging a donkey. It's a neat way to reclaim the feeling of feeling, of recapturing childlike warmth, of seeing yourself again staring out of the window on a rainy day, of embracing a creature who's simply *there*, who's whole. I wonder, too, whether we could rename the Myshkinian Primal Bray "Fleeing on a Donkey." By *fleeing*, I don't mean something negative or defensive; I don't mean running away or avoiding: I mean confronting, actively fleeing from the unreality Janov speaks of, refinding your true self, the real one, not the one you erect for worldly appearances, nor the one you're forever struggling against. By fleeing, then, I mean inwardly telling yourself: *No more! Enough, already!* It's time to let yourself be who you really are.

I've always thought that's why the American poet Anne Sexton wanted to "flee on a donkey," why she wanted a cathartic, curative release from the psychiatric institution that interned her, from the sad hotel she knew was the Great Depression of modern life. Sexton never quite made it onto a real donkey, out on the road, nor heard primal braying in the marketplace like Prince Myshkin.

That's too bad. Like her contemporary Sylvia Plath, Sexton was a wordsmith of great talent, a "confessional" poet who wrote stanzas of prodigious force and emotional honesty. She said she wrote her long poem, her brilliant long poem "Flee on a Donkey" in 1962, when she was institutionalized, drafted all 240 lines of it "in the nut house and rewrote it 98765432 times until this spring [1966] . . . Took me all those years to figure it out . . . Don't hurry it. There's no hurry. It's not a horse race."

A lot of people ask why Sexton called her poem "Flee on a Donkey" when it really isn't a poem about a donkey. They're missing something important: Sexton was rapping at the same psychological door as Dostoevsky's Prince Myshkin. He passed through it; she was fumbling for the keys, groping for the lock, trying to cross its primal threshold. Her hands trembled as she sought to satisfy her hunger for warmth, for innocence regained, for the unconscious and unself-conscious feeling of feeling. "Flee on a Donkey" represented a new poetics for Sexton, a new form of "writing about the unconscious," a defining moment in her art. Surely it wasn't entirely coincidental that a donkey was her chosen metaphorical mount, the selected holy animal to take her away, to help her flee her neurotic self?

She said she'd received a message from another tormented soul, the nineteenth-century French poet Arthur Rimbaud. It was a kinetic connection across a generational divide and storm-tossed ocean, voicing a desperate, rhyming plea, alas lost in its English translation: "*Ma faim, Anne, Anne, / Fuis sur ton âne.*" "My hunger, Anne, Anne, /

Flee on your donkey." (*Âne*, the French word for donkey, and Anne, the English name, share the same phonetics; and *faim*, i.e., hunger, is pronounced like the English *fan*, with a soft final "n": so, in Rimbaud's version, we have "*faim, âne* and Anne" all in rhyming unison.)

Sexton's fragile psychological disposition was long-standing, as were her suicidal tendencies. One analyst said her sole talent might be prostitution. Her poetry reflected a complex inner state and twisted self. Most times Sexton's poetry became the medium to externalize and rechannel her private thoughts and psychic impulses. For years she was in therapy. Apparently, during one sobbing session, Sexton reached into her pocket for a tissue and found a scrap of paper upon which Rimbaud's lines appeared; "my publisher sent Rimbaud to me," she explained, "in prose translation. I don't read French, but all of a sudden I saw my name—and the rest of the poem is about hunger."

Rimbaud's poem, written in 1872, was called *Fêtes de la Faim*—"Feasts of Hunger," and is almost framed in the donkey first person: "My hungers, turn away! My hungers, / Graze on fields of bran! ... The leaves are out across the earth! / I'm off for the flesh of softening fruit. / At the furrow's heart, I pick Lamb's lettuce and the violet." After Rimbaud, Sexton named her madness "a kind of hunger," a hunger that eventually starved her to death. She killed herself in 1974 at the age of forty-six, a combination of vodka and carbon monoxide poisoning, sitting in her garage, in her red 1967 Cougar, listening to the radio, wearing her mother's old fur coat: "a woman's way out," she called it, the "Sleeping Beauty."

Because there was no other place
to flee to,
I came back to the scene of the disordered senses,
came back last night at midnight,
arriving in the thick June night
without luggage or defenses, giving up my car keys and my cash,
keeping only a pack of Salem cigarettes
the way a child holds a toy.
I signed myself in where a stranger
puts the inked-in Xs—
for this is a mental hospital,
not a child's game . . .

Six years of such small preoccupations!
Six years of strutting in and out of this place!
O my hunger! My hunger!
I could have gone around the world twice
or had new children—all boys.
It was a long trip with little days in it
and no new places . . .

In here,
it's the same old crowd,
the same ruined scene.
The alcoholic arrives with his gold clubs.
The suicide arrives with extra pills sewn
into the lining of her dress.
The permanent guests have done nothing new.
Their faces are still small
like babies with jaundice . . .

This is madness
but a kind of hunger.
What good are my questions
in this hierarchy of death
where the earth and stones go
Dinn! Dinn! Dinn!
It is hardly a feast.
It is my stomach that makes me suffer.

Turn, my hungers!
For once make a deliberate decision.
There are brains that rot here
like black bananas.
Hearts have grown as flat as dinner plates.

Anne, Anne,
flee on your donkey,
flee this sad hotel,
ride out on some hairy beast,
gallop backward pressing
your buttock to his withers,
sit to his clumsy gait somehow.
Ride out
any old way you please!
In this place everyone talks to his own mouth.
That's what it means to be crazy.

Hearing the Primal Bray, motioning to its clumsy gait, letting your defenses drop, ridding yourself of what Janov calls "the unreal system," is a risky business: to be defenseless nowadays means being an idiot, a loser, a laughable creature—an ass, a Gribouille. Maybe we can try to laugh it off together, bray heartily, out loud, all be good-natured, like Prince Myshkin. I'm braying now, in my own funny kind of way, knowing what's happening to me, knowing what the prince knew and what Anne Sexton almost knew: that if we hug a donkey, if we enter its being, we can forget about being clever, forget about ourselves, forget about the self the world wants us to be. We can satisfy our hunger, feel a donkey's warmth, reach out to its innocence, watch our defenses tumble, become purer again. But fleeing on a donkey means more than taking a vacation and going for a walk. It means braying for life, braying for keeps. It means *bringing it all back home*, braying in everyday life, where it matters most.

35

THAT BIG BLUE'S bray, and Gribouille's follow-up, convinced me that I'm doing the right thing, convinced me that I am going to *bring it all back home*. Yes, I'm going to make my way back home, with Gribouille, take him into my own everyday life, just for a while anyway, until I give him back, return him. We're not too far now from our homecoming, from our Ithaca of the mind, our Eccles Street up on the hill, from petit Le Pouget. We're entering Jax, moving along a narrow tarmac road. We're passing a small field full of brown goats, with real goatees and gleaming coats and chains tinkling around their necks, and over there, on the horizon, look, Gribouille, we can see windmills, really see them, drawing us nearer to where we want to go. They're strangely beautiful beacons fluttering in the west wind. The world is down there, my friend, for our taking, within touching distance. Jax's village church has a gray conical bell tower and next to it I can see a wild boar, yes, a wild boar, carved out of wood, life-size, a life-size nonsmoker, a healthy immobile beast, hailing our passage along the roadside. We pass it and continue down the incline, descending into the valley.

It's funny, but everything seems clearer now, less murky, and things are speeding up, actually going faster, really fast. We're making progress. Gribouille and I are floating down the hill, effortlessly, as if our legs and hooves aren't touching the ground anymore, with immense grace and absolute weightlessness, watching the landscape enter us in a collapsing of distance, into the nearness of distance. We're drifting, a paraglider with a donkey; or am I hitching a ride with a paragliding donkey? We're floating through the clouds, soaring above the ground, like giant birds, two albatrosses waiting to be shot down. I glimpse a fuzzy outline of a hermit's donkey. Or maybe that's Gribouille I'm seeing, and maybe that hermit is me. We're like the Tao mystic Chang Kuo, from the Tang Dynasty, and his gleaming white donkey, his magic donkey, traveling thousands of miles every day. Kuo and his great white are over there, somewhere in the breeze, or else they're in us here, somehow in us.

Chinese folklore says Kuo had acquired the art of prolonging life, tapping some secret wisdom. Often he mounted his donkey backward, carrying a bamboo musical instrument called a "fish-drum." When he stopped, Kuo's donkey turned into paper and Kuo could fold him up and slip him into a cap box. As soon as he wanted to ride him again, Kuo moistened his origami fold, and it revivified as a donkey. And off they went once more. Like other human-donkey duos, Kuo and his donkey were inseparable; in fact, the association between the man and animal was so tight that when Kuo is portrayed without his mount, a miniature image of the donkey can be seen as a curling wisp of vapor, glowing out of the open end of Kuo's fish-drum sack. The primordial vapor lingers, the source of all life.

Gribouille's primordial vapor is lingering beside me. I feel its warming comfort, its vital life energy; I feel the force of fur. We're getting nearer. I can see the priory at Lavoûte-Chilhac, partly ruined, built in 1045, a Gothic vault and former monastery. And the Allier River next door, where it wends around and turns back on itself, flowing upstream. In the olden days it had giant salmon swimming in it, crammed full of them. It's all there below, the village and the priory, and the Allier, minus the salmon. Suddenly, we're back touching earth again, feeling our divine terrestrial calling, ambling across a narrow medieval bridge opposite the priory. It curves upward and we dip up and down with its span, over the Allier. I've got a hand on Gribouille's poll and he seems to know what's happening, where we're going. A few passersby recognize me, wave and shout *bonjour! Bonjour!* I rejoin.

Bon retour, I think to myself. The wanderer is returning, after years away; it seems like years away.

We pass the Café de la Tour and Le Prieuré hotel and restaurant, then *le pêcheur* bar and the Post Office and go along near the banks of the Allier, on the right bank, near the *boulodrome*. There are tall, narrow buildings lining the nonriver side, and we sneak behind them, take a back route, up a narrow medieval passageway between a tight row of houses; a few are abandoned, many are for sale, a handful more are bright and cared-for, with window boxes of fresh flowers and mailboxes that still take mail. We exit Lavoûte-Chilhac and take a small spiraling country lane, ascending a long incline with fields either side, rolling countryside, going slow again; clip-clop we motion, tap dancing for the final stretch, the Allier to the west. Then the expectation of a donkey in your midst: I suddenly start thinking about what it means to bring a donkey back home, back into your household. I glimpse a cluster of stone houses up there in the foreground, immediately ahead, capping the hilltop; and a little hamlet, *chez moi*. I know I'm arriving.

36

I'VE READ A lot about the therapeutic value of a donkey in the household, about how they can be a source of unconditional love, an outlet for expressing affection, particularly for kids who've had none; and how they can be long-eared teachers with calming properties, who instill relaxation, who aid juvenile attention retention, who re-create unity in households crippled by disunity. I'd even seen with my own eyes the remarkable effects of a donkey in the home, *literally* in the home, in a retirement home, alongside the elderly, doing a call of duty. I remember it as a tremendously moving experience. I can see one silvery moon now, with all the calm of Buddha, a little donkey called Lulu, standing there with all the poise of the patron saint of donkey tranquility, of donkey unflappability, with a neat crew cut throughout her body, specially sheared in order that she doesn't shed her coat on the carpet. Only her front stays fluffy, coiffed just right for patting. With her black leather halter, decorated with ears of corn, Lulu is one of the most elegant donkeys I've ever seen. It's impossible *not* to caress Lulu: she's an animal who is tactility incarnate, a comfort zone of languid warmth and patience.

She's creating a lot of attention in a room full of people, elderly people. It's perhaps not too surprising: a donkey indoors, in a spick-and-span human habitat, an admittedly curious sight, a shock for a few; others smile bewilderedly, not believing their eyes, laugh and then suddenly start to cry, tears rolling down their cheeks with joy. The atmosphere is emotionally charged. Everybody is *touched* by something, touched because of a donkey. It's hard to say exactly what it is. But it's really something to behold; you'll not forget it easily. Lulu, of course, takes everything in her modest little stride. We're standing around her at the Swallowcliffe Residential Home in Seaton, midway between Sidmouth and Lyme Regis, for the monthly visit of Sidmouth Donkey Sanctuary's School-Education and Therapy Unit, under the attentive eye of Jan Aherne, the project manager, who carries a flexible plastic bucket ready to be placed under Lulu's rear end— just in case. It's a retirement home dramatically overlooking cliffs, amid tropical palm trees. Not a bad location to end one's days.

Jan laughs and tells me about the plastic flexible bucket. It's a precaution she's never yet had to use: "Lulu is polite. She knows it's not proper to do it in a living room! It's funny, but she'll let you know if she ever needs the bathroom. She'll get fidgety and she'll swish her tail briskly. You know what she's telling you." Lulu isn't only calm; she's extremely intelligent, and toilet-trained to boot, with a sense of etiquette and good behavior. "She's beautiful," says Ria, an eighty-something denizen at Swallowcliffe, who's petting Lulu's brow and talking to the donkey like she'd talk to her own granddaughter. "Isn't she beautiful," Ria repeats.

I ask Ria what she likes most about Lulu. Ria reflects a bit and then says: "She's so placid . . . she's so placid, isn't she." Lulu is led around a communal room with several centenarians. They can all pat the star donkey and look into dark eyes that transmit calm as effectively as any sedative. The room comes alive and for a while residents forget the TV. "Lulu brightens up their day," Jan winks at me. "It's the same wherever we go.

She'll always start people talking, she always makes their day."

※

The Donkey Sanctuary's therapy unit, equipped with special blue touring truck for Lulu (including CCTV surveillance to keep an eye on her in transit), visits schools and retirement homes, hospices and rehab centers all over Devon two or three times a day, five days a week. "Bedbound kids with special needs, kids who've been withdrawn for years, suddenly utter words in the presence of a donkey, suddenly get stimulated and show affection," Jan says. "Elderly residents also, who've never moved, stand up from their chairs, or else exit their rooms when Lulu has appeared. I've seen these things all the time and it's very fulfilling. It's great to see people smiling, and Lulu loves it too, she loves being fussed over." "A donkey can have an amazing effect on people. Staff at retirement homes adore seeing a donkey as much as the residents."

We see it ourselves at the next stop, at the Dove Court retirement center, five minutes down the road. Lulu causes a stir with everybody when she enters. She's led into a private room where Tony, another octogenarian, sits up in bed, and wills the donkey to approach him. "Look at her," Tony says. "What a lovely girl." Tony breaks open a box of After Eight chocolates and offers Lulu one. "Come here, girl, take this . . ." Lulu accepts willingly, but knows how to take it gently from Tony's hands, knows how to go easy. Jan frowns and warns that with other donkeys you have to watch they don't inadvertently bite your hands when you offer food. Tony holds out another mint; Lulu gobbles it up in one swoop; and another, and another ... Lulu's having a fine time: she knows she's being mischievous, indulging in a little treat, and laps up the attention, flicks around her ears and casts a minty smile. You can smell chocolate on her breath if you get near. She's really licking her lips and dilating her nostrils.

Then Tony starts reminiscing about donkeys and the Second World War, when he was overseas in Italy ... Jan whispers to me that donkeys always act as "a sort of memory trigger"; they always prompt some story or another. It's fascinating to witness how donkeys activate the sense of touch as well as a sense of remembering. "A donkey's therapeutic value is incredible, and proven," Jan resumes. Donkeys are great facilitators of communication and tactile interaction; they're nonjudgmental and can be an emotional outlet. For the elderly, donkeys like Lulu with their kind and gentle ways, offer stimulation. "Donkeys are the source of conversation long after we've left," says Jan. "And they can help children learn about living creatures, adding a tactile perspective to the teaching of science and natural history. Our donkey school visits are met with enormous enthusiasm, from pupils and teachers alike."

Later that same afternoon I was in Jan's office at the Donkey Sanctuary talking about what we'd just seen in action: Animal Assisted Therapy, or AAT. It's now an officially recognized branch of medicine emphasizing the value of animals in promoting the social and psychological welfare of people. In 1929, it was discovered that when somebody strokes a dog, the animal's blood pressure drops; fifty years on, it was found that the blood pressure of that person doing the stroking equally drops, too. When people interact with animals, things happen to blood pressure and plasma cholesterol, to anxiety and stress levels: they reduce, favorably. One 1991 study from the *Journal of Nervous and Mental Disease* says: "animals can decrease anxiety and sympathetic nervous system arousal by providing a pleasant external focus for attention, promoting feelings of safety and providing a source of *contact comfort*."

The idea of "contact comfort" helps identify, at least in part, the joy of interacting with a donkey, the pleasure and comfort derived from rubbing the fluffy warm forehead of an animal so peaceably soft and placid, so gentle and so trusting. Something happens to us when you pet and pat an animal; it says a lot about us, too, about *our need to pet*, about our need to touch to help us stay alive, to help us know ourselves as sensuous beings. This yearning for contact comfort, for unmediated tactility, for being "skin hungry," has been medically acknowledged and scientifically measured. Touching a soft animal, being in its calm company, affects our neurotransmitters, increases the sensitivity of the brain's receptors, and so positively affects our emotional life. It augments our sense of wellbeing, lets us feel that a void, a psychological void, is getting filled.

Another study, from 1998, this time in the *Journal of the American Psychiatric Association*, investigated "the effects of Animal-Assisted Therapy on anxiety ratings of hospitalized psychiatric patients." "Statistically significant reductions in anxiety scores," the article notes, "were found after the animal-assisted therapy sessions for patients with psychotic disorders, mood disorders, and other disorders." Group sessions were organized around interactions with a dog that freely moved around the room, and a therapist encouraged discussion about patients' own pets and their interactions with canines and other animals.

Psychiatric patients hitherto withdrawn are described as reacting positively, with smiles and hugs and talking. Reductions in anxiety scores for patients with psychotic disorders are apparently twice as great after animal-assisted therapy as after therapeutic recreation. "Animal-assisted therapy," the study concludes, "may offer patients with psychotic disorders an interaction that involves fewer demands compared with traditional therapies. Perhaps the therapy dog provides some sense of safety and comfort not found in traditional inpatient therapies. Alternatively, the dog may provide a nonthreatening diversion from anxiety-producing situations. Or perhaps it is the physical touching of the dog that reduces patients' anxiety."

❧

The seminal Animal-Assisted Therapy study harks back to the early 1960s, to the New York child psychotherapist Boris Levinson, who wrote an intriguingly titled article in the journal *Mental Hygiene*: "The Dog as a 'Co-Therapist.'" Levinson knew he was provoking, knew he was challenging conventional therapy wisdom with a close-to-home discussion about his dog Jingles, eminently readable for a layperson like me. Yet there's something tellingly path-breaking in Levinson's unorthodoxy, in his tonality, and a lot stuck, stirred up the psychotherapy profession. In reading it, all I could think about was how a donkey like Lulu, or the red-haltered Gribouille, or Dapple and Platero, or the magus bringer of gifts Balthazar, might also be "cotherapists" in this healing voyage I'm embarked upon.

Levinson's dog Jingles is a loyal and affectionate chap, an unwitting therapist himself, who never needed zillions of dollars spent on his medical school education. He was there that day in Levinson's office, circa 1960, curled up on the floor at his master's feet, who was busy writing and awaiting his next appointment, an eight-year-old withdrawn boy—a problem case for a long while. The patient and parents arrived early—in fact an hour before scheduled—and Jingles suddenly ran over toward the child to lick him. "Much to my surprise," Levinson writes, "the child showed no fright but instead cuddled up to the dog and began to pet him."

The parents wanted to separate the two; Levinson signaled to leave the child alone. After a while the child asked about the dog and expressed a desire to play with Jingles. In subsequent sessions, Jingles stays in the room and the two play together. "Gradually," says Levinson, "as some of the affection elicited by the dog spilled over onto me, I was included in the play. We came slowly to the establishment of a good working relationship and to the eventual rehabilitation of this young boy." "It's anybody's guess," Levinson asks, "what might have been the child's reaction had the dog not been present that morning."

From that point on, Jingles was used with certain child patients, and the seeds of a new approach took root. A dog, Levinson thinks, can play numerous roles in relation to a child: a companion, friend, servant, admirer, confidant, scapegoat, mirror, and defender. When a child needs to love "safely," without fear of losing the loved one, without losing face, the dog fulfills this need. "When a child craves a close, cuddly, affectionate, nonjudgmental relationship, the dog can provide it. Dogs can't 'talk-back' when yelled at by a child. And no human being can offer to the child more general 'acceptance' in its fullest multi-ordinal levels of meaning, than a faithful dog, for whom the master can do no wrong." Levinson concludes: "It is the author's opinion that a greater understanding of the child's need for cuddling, love and affection, whether by animals or human beings, would lead to more rapid recovery in many children."

We might ask, of course, whether that need for cuddling rests exclusively with a child. Maybe it resides in adulthood as well, buried and repressed, sublimated into less peaceable activities, into more disturbing neuroses? Perhaps, then, an animal like a donkey, who can be cuddled and who listens without ever telling, without ever judging, is vital in our healthy mature development, in our grown-up emotional well-being? "Maybe some day," Levinson reflects, "we shall advance so far our understanding of animals and their meaning to human beings that we shall be able to prescribe pets of a certain kind for different emotional disorders. It seems to us that the type of pet one chooses is a reflection of one's personality." You have to wonder, too, don't you, how much Anne Sexton might have benefited from a Lulu visit, or from a voyage with Gribouille, from Gribouille Assisted Therapy; how much she might have benefited from that hairy beast as cotherapist she'd yearned for and wrote confessional poetry about. Sexton might have then ridden out, healed, with her buttocks pressed to a donkey's withers, from the New England "nuthouse" she'd found herself interred in.

Unlike Sexton, Prince Myshkin stumbled across his emotional release, his primal scream, his Animal-Assisted Therapy, in the presence of a donkey, and for a while experienced the rocky road toward self-maturation. He'd found his donkey cotherapist out in a Swiss marketplace, and shared his braying adventure with us on the page. And the earthy wisdom of Dapple, another successful covert cotherapist, another donkey confidant, taught Sancho Panza as much about the meaning of life and human folly, with all its loose ego boundaries, as did Don Quixote himself. It's a folly that society thrives off, dangles in front of us, compels us to participate in; and, like Sancho, most of us get sucked (and suckered) into this folly, pushed down this route where madness lies. Who doesn't have ambitions of fame and glory, of amassing wealth and fortune, of being governor of some island or another?

37

WE'RE STILL WINDING our way upward. Nearly home now. As we follow the bend, the road steepens abruptly before it levels off again for another stretch. Houses are getting closer, Gribouille, we can almost see the little blue-and-white sign announcing our arrival, an old sign beside the roadside, next to a pile of nettles overflowing from the hillside. I can see a massive shed on the right, with hay bales, and a ruined old house next door, whose roof has caved in and back wall collapsed. I can see a rotten bed within, exposed to the elements, and wardrobes and tables and a sewing machine, all looking like a decrepit, sick joke of a doll's house, only on a real-life scale. It reminds me, should I ever need reminding, that a lot is poor around here, raw somehow, that people's lives have caved in, that this is a dying as well as a living environment, not a showcase made for window-gazing, where only pretty looks count . . .

✿

The rich man's folly passes for good judgment in our world, said Sancho, in one of his greatest parables, voiced just before he fell afoul of the rich man's world. "In a few days," he wrote his wife Teresa, "I'll leave for the governor-ship, and I'm going there with a real desire to make money because I've been told that all new governors have this same desire." Sancho follows a long tradition in which knight-errants promise to install their squires in the gov-ernorship of a little kingdom somewhere. But in Sancho's case, as a practical joke, done at Don Quixote's expense, and perpetrated by the Duchess, the peasant squire is fast-tracked to his island governorship. "As for governing well," says Sancho in his vetting interview with the Duch-ess, "I'm charitable by nature and have compassion for the poor." And don't let looks deceive, appearances kid you, he adds, because often "under a poor cloak you'll find a good drinker."

The Duchess laughs at Sancho's simplicity, at a naïve wisdom she knows will come unstuck in the cynical arena of politics and economics. She grants Sancho his island; he kisses her hand and begs her to be so kind as to "give direc-tions about the entertainment of Dapple, who was the apple of his eyes." When she asks what he meant by Dapple, "'My ass,' replied the squire, 'whom, rather than use the vulgar term, I call Dapple.'" "Let Sancho take Dapple to his governorship," the Duchess says, "and there you can treat him as nicely as he wants, and even keep him from hard labor." Sancho reminds her grace that this shouldn't seem too remarkable, for, after all, "I've seen more than one or two asses go to governorships, and it'll be no new practice if I carry Dapple to mine."

Once in office, all sorts of tricks and connivances be-fall Sancho: A quack physician, on the Duchess's payroll, restrains him from eating anything "that will be hurtful and prejudicial to Sancho's stomach." Gone is spicy food, which increases thirst, and if you drink too much, says the doctor, it destroys sane reasoning; Sancho asks about the dish of juicy partridges, nicely seasoned, that roasts yonder, surely that won't harm? "A full stomach is bad, but a stomach full of partridges is very bad," insists the physician. "It is my opinion," he goes on, "that your grace shouldn't eat the rabbit stew over there either because that's a long-haired animal. You could have tasted the veal, if it hadn't been roasted and marinated, but it's out of the question now." And the big pot of sliced-ham and chicken casserole, how about that, wonders governor Sancho? That's only for peasant weddings, or for rectors of colleges, says the physician, never for the table of governors!

Meanwhile, starving Sancho has to pass judgment on shady petitioners who come to his court: some ask him for money, others to resolve marital disputes and domestic squabbles; again, they're all put up to it by the Duchess, all out to embarrass poor Sancho, to highlight his worldly incompetence. Ironically, rather than be a laughingstock, Sancho actually passes wise judgment and enacts bold, popular laws; each vassal and steward is impressed with the "Constitution of the Great Governor Sancho Panza." Don Quixote hears the good news: "They tell me you govern as if you were a man," he writes his former squire, "and that you are a man as if you were an animal, so humbly do you behave." Even so, Sancho is warned that spies, killers, and enchanters are in the midst, people who want to poison him, and overthrow his island. Then, on the seventh night of governorship, "full not of bread or wine, but of judging and giving opinions and issuing statutes and decrees," the Fall, or rather the Realization, arrives.

His aides awaken Sancho, amid the clamor of bells and trumpets, with news that enemies have invaded the island. "To arms, to arms, Señor Governor, to arms!" It's all a fabrication, of course, another practical joke, again staged by the Duchess, and everybody apart from Sancho is in the know. He's donned in armor so tightly fitted that he can't move a single step; he topples to the ground, unable to rise; he's trampled on like a giant turtle by a stampeding mob, and humiliated by the tricksters. "Oh, if only Our Lord would put an end to the loss of this island, and I would find myself dead or free of this affliction!"

Then, suddenly, somebody announces: "Victory, victory! The enemy is retreating! Oh, Señor Governor, your grace should get up and come and enjoy the conquest." In a dolorous voice, Sancho asks to be picked up. They help him to his feet. Bruised and battered, he begs them for wine, to wipe away the sweat, and to untie his armor. He faints from shock and alarm. "Those who had deceived him regretted having carried the joke so far, but Sancho's return to consciousness tempered the regret caused by his swoon." He asks them the time; they tell him dawn has just broken. He falls silent, and "without saying another word he began to dress, deep in silence, and everyone watched him, waiting to see what the outcome would be of his dressing himself so earnestly."

Then, having put on his clothes very carefully, for his bruises wouldn't permit speed, Sancho heads off, with everyone in his train, to the stable where Dapple awaits him; and so unfolds one of *Don Quixote*'s profoundest scenes, its climatic moment, though hardy ever acknowledged as such. Sancho advances toward Dapple and, upon reaching his old loyal partner, whom he'd temporarily abandoned, embraces him affectionately, "and gave him the kiss of peace upon his forehead, saying, while tears trickled from his eyes, 'Come hither, my dear companion, my friend and sharer of all my toils and distress; when you and I consorted together, and I was plagued with no other thoughts than the care of mending your furniture, and pampering your little body, happy were my hours, my days, and my years! But, since I left you and mounted on the towers of pride and ambition, my soul has been invaded by a thousand miseries, a thousand toils, and four thousand worries.' "

※

This scene, which I like to call the "Kiss of Peace" scene, the kiss Sancho gives Dapple in his stable, a gesture that seems the most anachronistic act for our bellicose age, has been immortalized by the great French illustrator Gustave Doré in an 1863 lithograph. Doré did a series of lithographs for Cervantes' masterpiece that all tend to revolve around Don Quixote himself, Gothic in style and typically black and white. Yet in the "Kiss of Peace" engraving, peasant Sancho and donkey Dapple get star treatment. A giant tear trickles down Sancho's face, down an agonized face, passionately emotive, so sun-tanned, lined, and leathery that it looks like a sun-dried tomato with a bulbous nose. Sancho's hair is curly jet-black, and he wears a rumpled peasant smock. His hands are big and callused, yet tender as they grip Dapple's muzzle, as he presses his grimacing face against the donkey's brow. Straw hangs out of Dapple's mouth, a mouth that almost smiles, and he's dribbling onto Sancho's chest. His ears rest on Sancho's head and his eyes stare out as only a donkey's eyes can stare out—calm, content, and wistful. Doré has captured the wisdom of donkeys and given us *the* most complete image we know of Animal-Assisted Therapy, of a donkey as cotherapist, one that will never be surpassed.

Dapple brought Sancho back to reality and became the symbol of a purity that Sancho had abandoned, momentarily, in his vanity and greed, in his thirst for wealth and ambition in a conceited world where all higher values are rendered meaningless, deemed naïve, even laughed at. (The Duchess was always *amused* by Sancho, and guffawed heartily at him and his donkey.) With Dapple—or rather *through* Dapple—Sancho experienced a shock of recognition, a Primal Scream, like Balaam seeing the angel his donkey had long before seen. Through Dapple, Sancho saw Kafka's "truth about Sancho Panza": that is, he saw the truth about himself, that he was a simple man, an honest man, with a simple donkey, honest and peaceable. At heart an ambitious cynic, Sancho was not. "Make way, gentlemen," Sancho says, after embracing Dapple, after rearranging his packsaddle for the road, "let me return to my former liberty: let me go in quest of my former life, that I may enjoy a resurrection from the present death."

"I'm better versed," he says on parting, "in plowing and digging, in pruning and planting vines, than in enacting laws and defending provinces and kingdoms ... I'd rather fill my belly with ordinary soup than undergo the misery of an impertinent physician who starves me to death. I'd rather solace myself under the shade of an oak tree in summer, and clothe myself in a sheepskin jacket in winter, being my own master, than indulge, under the subjection of a government, with Holland sheets and robes of sable." Thus Sancho learned, the hard way, what most people learn the hard way: that the promise of fame and fortune is invariably a *ruse,* a trick honest simple people like himself get lured into, a trick purported by our own dukes and duchesses, who nurture this ruse, who promulgate it, who advertise it on TV, who send its glossy leaflets to you through the mail. The ruse is promulgated as *the* grown-up world, as real reality, as the *only* reality. The unsuspecting often realize the ruse when it's too late, when they've come too far, when there's no kiss of peace to give anymore, when, saddest of all, they've lost their childlike wonderment. "There's no malice in Don Quixote," Sancho once said of his own master. "A child could convince him it's night in the middle of the day; and for that simplicity I love him with all my heart and couldn't leave him no matter how many crazy things he does."

Sancho was always a reluctant man for an official's job, was never really committed to the deceit the task necessitates. His honesty and curiosity, his goodwill, would have, in theory, made him a great leader, a fine governor, perhaps even an admirable president, though one, we know, never ever likely to go the distance in the "real world." Penniless he took office and penniless he resigned that office, quite the reverse, he says, of what is usually the case with departing politicians. "Now move aside and let me go," he bawls. Now he wants nothing more than a little barley for Dapple, and a piece of cheese and half a loaf for himself. "Make way, gentlemen, make way!" All the company embraced him, "and were in their turns embraced by the weeping Sancho, who left them equally astonished at his discourse, as at his resolute and wise determination." And so went ex-governor Sancho, the penniless man, the cured man, the free man, "who, between merry and sad, jogged along upon Dapple."

※

Make way, make way! Let me pass with Gribouille, the apple of my eyes. But there aren't really any crowds around here, because this is a tiny hamlet with only half a dozen houses and a few ruins, as I've said. And it's as tranquil as ever as we take the last turn, a sharp hairpin up a short steep incline, and there, on the right, is the house with the curving wall, the wall locals know it by, my house, a modest old farmhouse with brown shutters and an orange tile roof. I'm crossing its threshold now, going through the gate, onto the lawn, when suddenly my wife appears out of the front door, beaming a smile, with tears of joy streaming down her face. She's jubilant at seeing me, at seeing Gribouille, at seeing me with a donkey. Red-eyed she steps forth, and, bearing our first child in her womb, hugs me, kisses me, and then, approaching Gribouille, the big chocolate brown, gives him the kiss of peace on his frizzy front, the curative response for the ills of our world. He stands there with those great, wondrous sad eyes, calm as anything, deadpan to it all. Then we all hug one another; and, as we get tangled up in Gribouille's soft floppy ears, his warm baguettes, I know, somehow I know, that this is as far as it goes, as deep as we can reach, as good as it gets . . .

38

THOSE TWO DAYS with Gribouille in our backyard were sweet and dreamy. Summer seemed to return even as fall approached, and our valley bathed in a crystal peace, in a serenity of a paradise found, one perhaps never quite lost. A golden halo shimmered over Gribouille as he grazed quietly on our little sloping meadow. In the next-door field, the neighbor's cows, *limousine* cows, wandered over curiously, staring at our guest, and offered the occasional moo of recognition, of shy fraternity. Everybody swished tails in mutual contentment.

I put up a temporary enclosure for Gribouille using taped portable fencing, which threads through a series of white plastic stakes that you can drive into the earth, making a space as big or as small as you need. The patch I've got here is too small as a permanent base for a donkey, yet the turf is rich and long enough for munching and for a while will suffice. I've sectioned him off from my wife's treasured vegetable garden, now overflowing with the fruits of her labor, goodies I know Gribouille *would* wolf down. I'll clear away his dung, his organic fertilizer, after he's gone, and pile it on the compost. He'll help nourish a future crop: Gribouille's crop.

Out back, sitting on our wooden deck, on our outside *terrasse,* in full glorious sunshine, I spy on Gribouille nosing around in the grass twenty yards away. I'm listening again to the soothing shuffle of donkey, a familiar sound, a safe sound. I smell the sweet scent of September earth mixed with the mild vapor of donkey. Sometimes he'll look up and over and stare in my direction. He stands transfixed, just looking, just assessing. Then he pulls away and resumes his own private doings, and his muzzle again scours the earth. When a ray of sunshine strikes him, his fur glistens like an incandescent coat of arms.

From my perch, I watch him framed against the entire valley, looking at the hills toward Ally, toward the west, at the rolling mountains to the south, and at Lavoûte-Chilhac directly below, an unbroken panorama of half-green, half-blue, a split-screen projection of land and sky. If I look hard enough, I can catch a glimpse of the tips of a twirling windmill, apparently buried in an upland meadow, semisubmerged, rotating in a windless breeze. I'm like a solitary onlooker surveying the scene of a Millet painting, Jean-François Millet, van Gogh's chosen master; Millet who spent summers in the Auvergne between 1866 and 1868, Millet who painted a rustic idyll, yet who depicted its harsh reality, its back-breaking labor, its hay-makers and fruit-pickers, its gleaners and sowers. Millet also had a keen eye for working donkeys, which he'd develop from little miniature pencil sketches, beautiful treasures done on vellum paper. Gribouille reminds me of one I once saw in Paris's Musée d'Orsay, Millet's study of a donkey, doodled in crayon from various angles, with different versions of its tail and ears and hind legs, all done with astonishingly simplicity: *Trois Études d'âne pour le Départ pour les champs.*

I hear the gentle sonority of a tractor plowing a field and watch it snaking a trail in the soil, going around and around. It's distant enough to harmonize with the birds' chorus and with the priory's bells. Together, they bring on a heavy-eyed afternoon slumber. Then a flash, a streak of fiery orange, ignites next-door's field, a red squirrel sprinting from one tree to another, between the cows, a cartoonlike squirrel with his happy tail flowing behind him. It's the sprint of victory, of freedom, of the country-side unbound. One time, in a past life, in a life faraway from this sleepy one before me, I yearned to take the A train to the center, to the heart of action I was terrified to miss, to a center that always lay elsewhere; now I'm happy being stationary, content no longer having to move, no longer seeking any action, daydreaming next to a D-road headed nowhere.

In Gribouille's presence, my whole life has passed before me. He's given me a chance, perhaps a second, for-tuitous chance, to analyze it, to leave what I want behind, to bury the dead, to go on living, to anoint it all, including all that follows, our unknown future, with the healing balm of hope, with the creative powers of imagination. He and I have shared stories together, communed our tale like Marie and Balthazar, conjoining the stages of a donkey's life with that of a human's, just like Robert Bresson did. I've somehow seen the pangs of childhood, its joys, its momentary joys, relived through a donkey's eyes; then the lost innocence, the mindless acts that constitute "normal" working life, ordinary daily madness; and, later, of sprinting to daylight, like that red squirrel, in middle age, where I am now, when I can at last see with clarity, when I can cast off grown-up cynicism. Under Gribouille's watchful eyes, I've glimpsed a lost purity, and reclaimed and regained it in my own head, passively . . .

Every once in a while, my wife strolls over to Gribouille, refills his bucket of water from the garden hose, and gives him a little pat. It's interesting because normally she's somebody who loathes touching animals, all types, and who fears and avoids them. But she says he's so adorable that he makes her feel calmer and more patient about stuff. He's a calming spirit to have around the household; even looking at him slows you down, has you worry less about your woes, about all the tasks you haven't *yet* done. And inside the house, when you can't see him, but when you know he's there outside, poking around, things mysteriously assume a more patient air, seem more measured and precise, more restful. He helps us deal with our daily irritable impatience; with him we struggle against its destructive edge, curb our needless haste. His sway is everywhere, his watchful, sorrowful eyes keep tabs.

His wisdom gets internalized, enters into you; it happens without seemingly happening.

Yet behind that calm and patience, beyond the tranquility, here is an animal who has been through rough times, who has suffered and knows about tragedy and pain. A donkey doesn't so much accept its cruel fate as bears it, lets it pass over them. They're the most philosophical of all animals, much more philosophical about their fate than human beings. And it's an instinctive philosophy, a stoic acceptance, a kind of beautiful strength, passive rather than aggressive, not an ugly violent power. Needless to say, their philosophy isn't academic, isn't read in books or taught in a privileged classroom: it's everyday, a simple disposition that's lived out and practiced, in an open field. We might say, if we used philosophical-speak, that a donkey's philosophy is *ontological,* that it's all about *Being,* the philosophy of permanent reverie, of daydreaming in the open air.

Donkeys know about moments of joy and happiness, about finding the perfect dandelion and a quiet meadow in the sun where a pal can scratch their back; but they know, too, how cudgels and goads abound everywhere, reside over the next hill, just around the corner, wielded by somebody who's always scheming nearby. Always. Thus, the future might be full of cudgels and goads—you never know what's in store; but then there's that quiet meadow somewhere, too, and it's *that* that keeps a donkey going: the taste of another dandelion, of a few young tender leaves to chew, on the sunny side of the hill.

One of the greatest exponents of this wisdom, hence

one of the greatest donkey philosophers, is Old Benjamin of *Animal Farm*, who casts a telling eye on the perplexing two-legged world. He never forgets anything, does Old Benjamin, remembers what went on before in history, every detail during his long life; and he knows that things never have been, nor would ever likely be, much better: "hunger, hardship, and disappointment being, so he said, the unalterable law of life."

Benjamin struggles on with life in the same slow, quiet, obstinate way, never siding with any faction, never shirking from toil, yet never volunteering either. He refuses to be persuaded by cant or seduced by rhetoric; and, in spite of everything, he remains his own donkey, guarding loyally his own independent self. At the same time, Old Benjamin never gives up hope. He hopes against hope, hopes about keeping going, about seeing the sunrise and the sunset for another day; and never, not even for an instant, not even when it would be an easier option, does he lose the dignity of being a lowly honest donkey.

39

WE HAD TO give Gribouille back, Gribouille the great philosopher, the nemesis of our frantic age; of course we had to give him back. We couldn't keep him forever; we couldn't part him from his chums in Allègre, or from his owner Jean, who lives in the old center of town, in a big gray building with twenty-odd rooms. It used to be a convent and I can see it now, just ahead on the right, as I walk with Gribouille, for almost the last time, for old time's sake, up a cruel hill, up a clip-clopping narrow cobblestoned street, the street from where we'd started out, oh so long ago now. The nuns left in 1970, and in recent years the site has been Jean and Anne-Marie's place of welcome for footloose travelers, as well as a permanent base for their "*Âne-en-Auvergne.*" Jean is as happy to see Gribouille return as my wife was sad to watch him depart. She hugged him for what will likely be a final hug, and gave him another kiss of peace to watch over him, and to watch over us. We'll need it. Then he and I strode off together over the horizon, embarking on a donkey odyssey, because this time it was *his* homecoming, a donkey's triumphal return.

I'd tied Gribouille to the gates of the courtyard, because Jean invites me in for apple juice and a chat. He wonders how it all went. Where to begin? What to say? If I had time, of course, I could recount what I've just recounted to you. But I wonder if Jean knows all this anyway; it was him who'd told me, after all, in our initial conversation together, months ago, that "after you've had an encounter with a donkey on a walking tour, had real contact with one, you're never the same. You're somehow touched forever." I plead guilty: I am touched forever, and perhaps that's all I need to tell him.

Why don't you walk Gribouille back to his field, Jean says, for one last doodle together. So off we go, for the final walk, the last waltz together, the final donkey tap dance, through familiar little back streets, onward to a field

Gribouille knows so well, where his friends await him. As we walk, side by side, I remembered again our first meeting, the first time I set eyes on Gribs, as I sometimes affectionately call him, when Jean and I had stopped at an empty field—or what I thought was an empty field. I remembered Jean parking his car and the sound of braying ringing out from behind the bushes, and the mad rush of donkeys on the move.

We're reaching this field again, a lifetime later, and I'm unbolting the lock to its entrance. I've taken the red halter off—I'll never do it again—and Gribouille runs into his enclosure, already forgetting me. Three other donkeys trot over, greet him, and they all merrily rub noses together. Then Gribs lies down in the earth and rolls and rolls, gives a victory roll, showing me once again that glowing white belly, his legs all tucked up, back in his protective womb. He has returned to his own bed, and that patch of bare, grassless meadow he rolls in is surely his very own. Welcome home, Gribs! I was overcome with a tremendous elation at returning him there, safe and sound, and happy to see him lying down with friends. But as I turn to walk away, I feel terribly lonely, am hit with an inconsolable sadness, a private grief, and can't hold back the tears. My eyes quickly mist up, get clogged with the sort of white sleep you sometimes get in the mornings upon waking...

It was nice to have had a friend, to have been tamed, to have created links, like the fox did with the Petit Prince. And even though the fox was sad the day the Petit Prince left him, the friendship was still worth the pain of their parting. It was a strange kind of *happy* sadness, I know it now, a weird sense of loss; not like a death, not like watching a donkey die, like Balthazar sitting so peacefully among the little lambs of the mountain meadow, all of whom gather around as his head droops closer and closer to the earth, as his eyes grow heavier and heavier in the deepest sleep he'll sleep, and as a few gentle chords of Schubert's piano begin to play. No, it was the sadness of moving on, of knowing something has just given way, of feeling like a loved one is going away for a while, perhaps going away forever, but that I can still write, still stay in touch, and I'm happy for them anyway, happy they want to leave. And I can always listen to Schubert any time I want, on CD, and that I'll never forget Gribouille or the adventures we've had together, or what he taught me, or how he felt. I'll always be able to close my eyes, touch his warm fur, reach out for his soft poll, hear his quiet sighing, and listen to the gentle piano of Schubert—the "sad one"—hear it playing in my head, beating in my heart ...

40

A COLD WIND whooshes in my ears. I'm listening into a giant conch, hearing the green sea. I hear its waves, in both ears, freewheeling down the hill. What's wonderful about going uphill is that sometime you've got to come down. I'm hunched over the handlebars, flying along like a downhill skier on fresh snow, the season's first. It's arrived already, a couple of light sprinkles, a hint of what's to come soon. And I've been out preparing, cutting up firewood with a chainsaw, slicing up loose logs of oak and beech, arranging them all into neat stacks of little *bûches*, each about a foot in length so they can fit in the stove. The wetter ones I'll burn next winter. Pieces with thick perimeters need to be whacked with an ax, along the grain. It's tough yet satisfying work, and it takes me several days to cut and stack everything; always it leaves me with aching arms, painful shoulders, and a stiff neck.

You feel the glorious moment of impact; you know instinctively when the hit is clean, when you've become at one with your swinging ax, when you're at peace with the gesture of cutting. The clean cut is a philosophical as well as a physical act of chopping, a harmonious mastery of a tool: the art of trying without trying, the strength of nonstrength. It shouldn't be an aggressive jerk made by an aggressive jerk. I always delight at the split, at the wood tumbling into two parts, and how each morsel will later burn in the living room, how the flames will dance wildly behind the stove's little pane of glass, how I'll stare at them, poke them with a poker, feel their sweet heat, stir them up into something at once intimate and universal. To stoke up the fire, said Gaston Bachelard, is to stoke up the universe, to tap a higher realm, something cosmic.

I pedal and see my breath as I look through the fog across the Allier valley. Donkeys should be indoors by now, sheltered, tucked away for the winter. Gribouille will

be huddled around his friends in a warm corner somewhere. You need to brake hard around sharp bends, but
not too hard, otherwise you'll slide on the damp asphalt.
You need to take heed of the motorists who expect nobody
else on the road, and who speed and cut corners. And since
you can't hear who's coming up behind either, you need to
hug the right flank tightly. After my accident, I'm still nervous about being back on my bike. I was off on a ride, not
long after returning Gribouille, when I'd seen a donkey
and a horse in a field. I couldn't resist taking a peek at this
gray donkey, sitting down in the sunshine, in an enclosure
beside the Cronce River, which now flows only like a big
stream. So I descended a steep, short ramp with two
trenches, shaped by the comings and goings of a tractor. In
winter, each trench is pliable thick mud; in summer,
they're dried up and rock-hard.

Down into the field I went, onward through the grass
toward the lower field with the donkey. He was basking in
the sunshine, oblivious to my presence, sitting up in his
blue halter. The horse bounded over, up to the fence, jeal-
ous of the attention I was plainly giving the donkey. For a
while, I sat on my saddle watching the donkey's tail thud
against the ground, shooing away the flies. The horse trotted friskily back and forth, wanting me to look; the donkey couldn't care less. I must've been miles away when it
happened, miles away in the clouds, daydreaming about
something other than riding a bike, because remounting
the ramp I lost momentum, pedaled as if I was asleep,
without sufficient force, and hit the side of the trench;
not having time to release myself from the lock-in pedals,

I tumbled *with* the bike into a briar patch, like a sprawling human Bre'r Rabbit.

I couldn't get up at first. My head was down at the lower end of the slope and the bike was somehow on top of me. Each time I tried to push myself up, I reached down into spiky bramble. Ouch! But when I did finally struggle free, I realized the problem wasn't so much scraped arms as an unsuspecting coldness: a deep wound in my calf, a massive chunk of flesh ripped off, likely by a pedal, with all the innards of my leg dangling out like mangled intestines; blood was dripping everywhere. I made it pedaling on one leg for a couple of miles, on the flat, until a passing motorist, recognizing the damage, stopped and gave me a ride home with my bike in the trunk. I eventually drove myself to Brioude hospital, hardly able to press the accelerator, for fifteen stitches and a lot of subsequent pain and hobbling.

It still hurts when I pedal hard up an ascent. Being hampered with a bad leg, though, willed me to sit tight and reflect upon the voyage I'd just done. I remembered the strange feeling I'd had that night after returning Gribouille, after coming home *without* a donkey. We'd shared one another's company for so long that his sudden absence brought on a longing. For what, I know not, exactly. My wife felt it as well. We both felt a bit lost, a bit downbeat, felt an unaccompanied quietness in the house. It lasted several days. During which time we moped around, talking about little else than missing Gribouille, wondering how he was doing, where he was . . .

But steadily, ever so steadily, this longing turned into a kind of pride, and a gratitude; not pride in ourselves, not a human vanity, but pride in Gribouille, pride of having spent time with him, of having learned from him, of having had donkeys in our midst; and a gratitude for them being simply what they are, for Gribouille simply being Gribouille. Henceforth I knew that the unfathomable donkey gaze would somehow appear less unfathomable, that the surety of their little legs would inspire surety in my little legs, that the stoic tranquility of their demeanor would become my stoic tranquility, that their peaceful spirit would inspire my peace. It would also help me come to terms with the Balaams who prowl our earth and who try to steer *me* along *their* path.

As the weeks passed, as the snow came, our time together became ever more make-believe, ever more otherworldly; the reality of our encounter became ever more *sur*real, better than real, above it: an imagined life form. How long had we walked together? A week, a month, a year, a few hours, forever? It's impossible to say with any clarity now. Had it really happened? Has it really ended? Indeed, is there really an end to a life walking with a donkey? Didn't Robert Louis Stevenson warn that we're all travelers with a donkey, travelers in the wilderness of the world? That wandering we did, or might have done—I'm no longer sure—that journey across Auvergne space, whatever it was, escaped all sense of time we know through clocks and calendars, through hours and minutes and days, through time as a measurable entity, as a linear category. All of it lost its meaning, its specific gravity, floated away into a depthlessness and timelessness, into somewhere beyond time, beyond space.

Maybe Spinoza would have said we'd been traveling with our donkey for an *eternity*, that with our donkey we'd discovered eternity, found an eternal moment—a moment when everything around us, the whole physical and natural world, flowed through us, became immediately palpable, touchable to us. In eternity, Spinoza said, "there is neither *when*, nor *before*, nor *after*," only *now*. Eternity is never defined by time, nor does it have any relation to time; it enters us through our mind, through the mind that feels those things it conceives, that finds its freedom in detachment and slowness, in passionate inwardness. And yet the curious thing about the eternal is that it also reveals the *finitude* of life, that eternity is really a finite infinity, that one day you get old and die, and it's that that makes the *eternal now* so precious and meaningful, so worthy of clinging on to. Soon it may be too late: now must be forever.

In the end, if indeed there is an end, encountering donkeys has helped me encounter myself, helped me understand a turning point. I'm no longer the same person I was before embarking on this book, on this trip. It's given me time and space, a green-and-white space, to reflect upon my life, to give up the ghost, to accept it all as a *fait accompli*. Now, it's today and today and today. And perhaps tomorrow. Or, if I really feel lucky, maybe it's the day after tomorrow, too. I can't think any farther ahead. I'm older now, a lot older, more content, wiser in a more naïve sort of way, more accepting of finitude, more philosophical about what lies ahead, about how long that finitude might be. Meantime, feeble cudgeling isn't going to break my back. Not ever. I'll struggle on, no matter what, despite the cold I feel this afternoon, despite the endless work of keeping this life afloat. The struggle never stops, of course; finding the eternal moment, retaining it, cherishing it, is, as Spinoza warned, hard to do, "as difficult as it is rare." This struggle is here and nowhere else now, a struggle with myself, within myself, a perpetual dialogue. I hope it's always going to be *now* now, that I'll have only this one eternal moment to live out, to perpetually struggle for.

There's whooshing in my ears again, cold air coming through in waves, a comfortable numbness in my feet as I freewheel through the fog. I wonder whether I've daydreamed it all up, imagined it riding my bike, and that it's still summer up the hill where I'd started out, watching those chocolate browns and turtledove grays graze on a slope in the calm of the world. Sometimes I even wonder if I really ever left New York, and that I'm still sitting on the number 2 express train, going downtown, staring at my feet, avoiding eye contact, smelling sweaty bodies and waiting for crowds of people to pile on at Times Square. Mind the gap! Hum ha? Is this a vision? Is this a dream? Do I sleep? In *The Tempest*, Shakespeare has Prospero say "we are such stuff as dreams are made on, and our little life is rounded with a sleep." But I can't help think that daydreams make us, that our little life is rounded with reverie rather than sleep, and that daydreaming—even about donkeys—no matter where you're sitting, no matter what tempest besets you or shipwreck befalls you, never harmed anyone. Least of all yourself.

ACKNOWLEDGMENTS

THIS SOLITARY FLIGHT of fancy had a lot of help from others, even from a few humans. Wendy Keller, my agent, encouraged, prodded, had faith in me when few did, and was tireless in her support for this book. Thank you, Wendy, for helping my inner voice find the page and talk back in ink. Michele Lee Amundsen, my editor, understood the project and shaped up the manuscript with enthusiastic good cheer and a keen eye. Jean Daudin's passion for donkeys was infectious and taught me much. Ditto Ben Hart at the Sidmouth Donkey Sanctuary, who was generous with both his time and equine expertise. Big thanks to Dawn Vincent and Amanda Gordon for making my visit to Sidmouth so memorable; thank you, Dawn, for encouraging me to go to Egypt where Dr. Mohsen proved more inspiring than the Pyramids. Less obvious, though no less important, has been the support of relatives in England, of my father, Nicolas and Peta-Jane, Camilla and Howard, and of friends in New York and France, of Neil, Eric and Barbara, David and Haydee, Jeff and Denisha, Steve and Susan, of Marie-Hélène and Vincent, David and Angelique, Yves and Madeleine, Pierrette and André, Maurice and Suzette, Alexandra, Agnès and Hervé, Alexandre and Eléonore, Ginny and Andrew. And, of course, without the input of Corinna, the love of my life, my most trenchant critic and tenderest reader, this little book would have been a great deal littler.

A NOTE ON THE AUTHOR

Born in Liverpool, England in 1960, Andy Merrifield taught geography for over a decade in assorted British and American universities. He's the author of four previous books, including biographies on two twentieth-century French philosophers. He now lives with his wife and young daughter in a small rural community in France's Auvergne region.